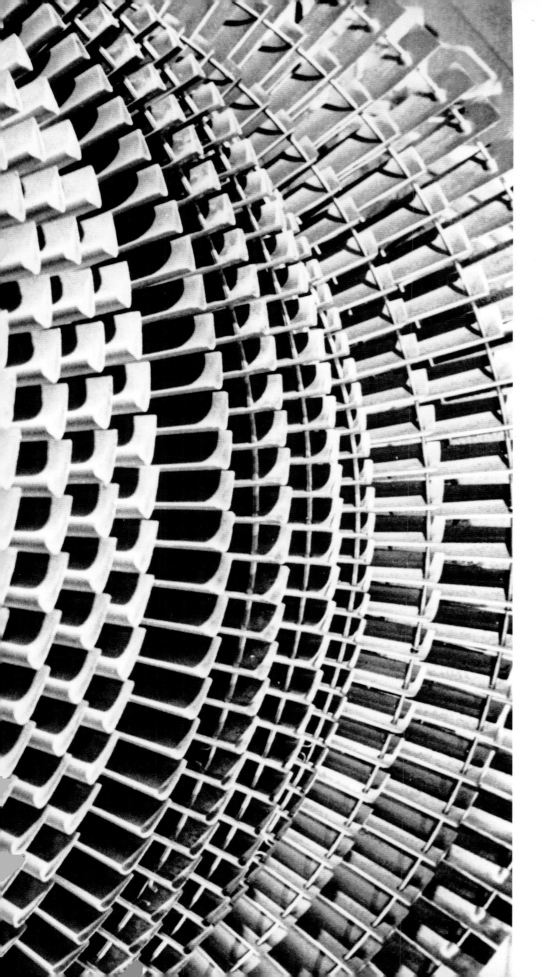

Candles to Kilowatts

The Story of Edmonton's Power Company

DEBBIE CULBERTSON
HEATHER MARSHALL

DUVAL HOUSE
PUBLISHING
LES ÉDITIONS DUVAL

Duval House Publishing Inc.

18228 – 102 Avenue

Edmonton, Alberta T5S 1S7

Ph: (780) 488-1390

Tollfree: 1-800-267-6187

Fax: (780) 482-7213

Website: http://www.duvalhouse.com

National Library of Canada Cataloguing in Publication Data

Culbertson, Debbie, 1959-
Candles to kilowatts

Includes bibliographical references.
ISBN 1-55220-293-3

1. EPCOR Utilities--History.
2. Electric utilities--Alberta--Edmonton-
-History. 3. Electrification--Alberta--
Edmonton--History. 4. Public utilities--
Alberta--Edmonton--History.
I. Marshall, Heather, 1956- II. Title.
HD9685.C34E62 2002
333.793'215'09712334
C2002-910030-5

Picture Credits

Every effort has been made to identify and credit all sources. The publisher would appreciate notification of any omissions or errors so that they may be corrected. All images and exceprts are copyright © of their respective copyright holders. Reproduced with permission.

t=top, b=bottom, r=right, l=left

City of Edmonton Archives
cover front and back, i, iii, iv, 2, 3t, 5, 7, 12, 13 (all but m), 16, 18b, 20, 21 (all), 22 (all), 23, 25, 26, 27, 28 (all but ml), 30 (all), 32, 33, 34, 35 (all), 40 (all), 42, 43, 44 (all), 47, 48, 50, 51, 54 (all) 55, 56, 58, 60, 63, 65, 67t, 68b, 70, 71, 72, 74 (all), 75, 77 (all), 82t, 91 (all), 95br, 95 (all), 96t
National Archives of Canada
3b: Charles W. Mathers/National Archives of Canada/C-005606
13m: Ernest Brown/National Archives of Canada/C-007911
Provincial Archives of Alberta
4 (all), 8, 11, 18t, 19, 31, 37, 45b, 92
Raylew Enterprise Ltd.
103t, 104bl
Edmonton Journal
(Ed Kaiser)104t, (Ed Kaiser)104br, (Chris Schwartz)105b
Heather Marshall
14, 82b, 88b
Bill Mayko
81t
George Faulder
69
All other photographs provided by EPCOR, EPCOR staff, or organizations associated with EPCOR.

Text Permissions

The Edmonton Journal has granted permission to reprint all *Edmonton Journal* articles included in this book that the *Edmonton Journal* owns copyright to.

Text excerpt on page 2(tl) reprinted with kind permission of the Canadian Electricity Association.

Text exerpt on page 11 reprinted with kind permission of Tony Cashman.

Text excerpt on page 39(br) reprinted with kind permission of Transalta Utilities.

The CJCA broadcast on page 41 reprinted with kind permission of CJCA Radio.

The CFRN broadcast on page 59 reprinted with kind permission of CFRN-TV.

Project Sponsors

The Edmonton Power Historical Foundation would like to thank the following organizations for sponsoring this project:

Gold Sponsor:

Alstom Canada, Mississauga

Bronze Sponsors:

Strategies and Tactical Technology Inc., Edmonton

Pemco Construction Ltd., Edmonton

Optiplan System Inc., Montreal

Donations were also received from:

John T. Boyd Company, Denver, Colorado

Steeplejack Services Group, Edmonton

Acknowledgements

Many thanks to the City of Edmonton Archives, which provided access to the letters, reports, and newspaper articles reproduced in this book.

The publishers would like to thank Lyn McCullough, who conducted many staff interviews included in this book.

The Edmonton Power Historical Foundation would like to thank Mildred (Lee) De Blieck for giving this book its name.

Edited and designed by David Strand

We acknowledge the financial support of the Government of Canada through the Book Publishing Industry Development Program (BPIDP) for our publishing activities. **Canadä**

Prologue

*I*t is difficult to say exactly when the idea to produce a history of the City of Edmonton's electrical utility was born, but the project really started in the late 1990s. A small team of (then) Edmonton Power employees, proud of their company and its history, felt compelled to capture some of the utility's past and store it within these covers.

The assembled team, consisting of members of the Edmonton Power Historical Foundation, first met in October 1997 to begin formulating ideas. It was agreed that the finished product should be, at the same time, informative and entertaining. In short, a coffee-table publication full of factual and anecdotal information. I believe that we have met our objectives, and trust that you agree.

At this point, I wish to give thanks to all my team members who have given up their time and energy to search the databases – mental, written, and photographic – for the elements that Debbie Culbertson and Heather Marshall then moulded into readable material. The team members were Art Baird, Paul Collis, Rhonda From, George Knowles, Lyn McCullough (our roving mike), Bob Swift, Dave Walker, Jim Weiss, and many others who assisted in research. Our gratitude is also extended to Glenn Rollans and David Strand, who were instrumental in pointing us in the right direction.

The story you are about to read is one of immense foresight. This utility depended on skilled and courageous leadership to bring it through difficult times and periods of great growth and innovation. It benefited from many talented managers, from Alex Taylor, who introduced the magic of electricity to a privileged few in 1891, to the many managers and City councils who led the utility after the Town of Edmonton purchased the fledgling generating station in 1902. Today, foresight and courage remain among the company's assets as it expands beyond the city walls.

The story does not end in 2002, as it seems from this book. What you have in your hands is merely a 100-year snapshot in the history of an organization that has more promise, and brighter future outlooks, than it ever has.

Ken Warren, chair
Edmonton Power Historical
Foundation Book Committee

Introduction

A century of growth and development, innovation and challenge is almost as difficult to transform into text as it is to generate electricity from fossil fuels. How do you condense facts and anecdotes into readable prose without losing the essential elements? How do you transmit the vision of electrical pioneers and politicians, the dedication of countless employees, and the experiences of customers over the decades via lines of type on a page?

A variety of information sources were required in order to produce this historical record. Months of mining provincial, city and company archives, visiting generating stations and substations and even touring an underground vault were involved. It entailed interviewing retired and current employees and attending annual general meetings and historical foundation meetings. The history of Edmonton's power company is about more than generating stations or transmission and distribution systems. It is about the people who made the decisions and the people who carried them out. It is about interactions with politicians and with customers.

The history of Edmonton's power company is closely connected to the history of the city itself. In fact, it existed before Edmonton was incorporated as a town. A mutually beneficial relationship developed between Edmonton and its power company; Edmonton's growth resulted in increasing demands for electricity, and the availability of electricity allowed Edmonton to develop.

The citizens of Edmonton purchased their power company back in 1902; alternatives to public ownership have since been considered many times, even in recent history. As late as 1999,

Edmonton City Council was grappling with the question of whether or not to sell the utility. As in the past, council decided to keep the utility as a municipally owned corporation, and to grow the business into the new millennium.

Another constant throughout the century has been the utility's drive to be on the leading edge of technological innovations. The Rossdale Power Plant, the generating station that has been located in Edmonton's downtown river valley throughout the city's history, boasted one of the world's first 10,000-kW turbogenerators in 1928. In 1931, Rossdale had the largest steam boiler in Canada. By 1941, it was Canada's largest thermal plant. When Rossdale was converted to natural gas in the late 1950s, the new turbine units were the largest of their kind to be installed in Canada at the time. The Clover Bar station, built in the 1970s, was the first power generating facility in North America to have a spring-supported foundation table installed beneath the turbine generators.

This tradition of innovation and leadership continues to this day. Edmonton's power company is now the only Alberta company to be involved in every aspect of power generation, transmission, distribution, and sales. It also sells water to Edmonton and 40 surrounding communities. The utility is also expanding into British Columbia, Ontario, and Washington State, and has assets valued at over two billion dollars. That's quite a switch from a little light and power company that provided service to a seven-block stretch of downtown Edmonton after sunset and from 5:30 AM until sunrise in the winter. A century later, the sun still hasn't set on this company.

Debbie Culbertson is an Alberta writer, editor, and researcher. She is currently working on a biography of Roberta MacAdams.

Heather Marshall is an Alberta writer, editor, and adult educator.

Table of Contents

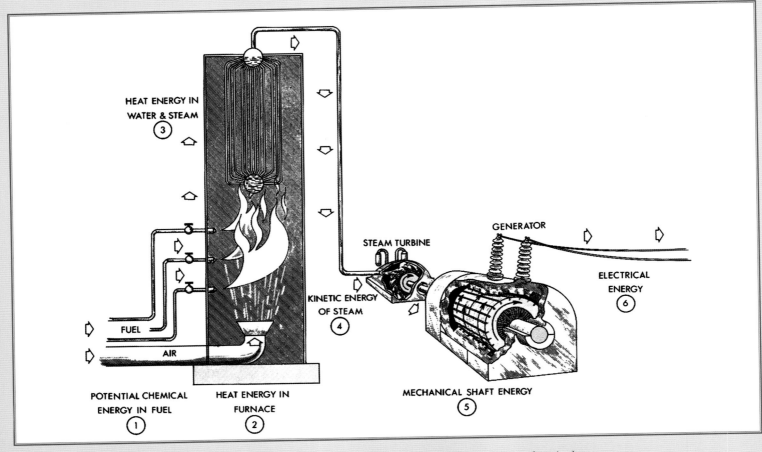

HEAT ENERGY IN
WATER & STEAM
③

STEAM TURBINE

GENERATOR

ELECTRICAL
ENERGY
⑥

KINETIC ENERGY
OF STEAM
④

FUEL

AIR

POTENTIAL CHEMICAL
ENERGY IN FUEL
①

HEAT ENERGY IN
FURNACE
②

MECHANICAL SHAFT ENERGY
⑤

A steam-driven power plant converts potential chemical energy into electrical energy.

CHAPTER I

Edmonton Electric Lighting and Power Company Limited

. . . . .

1891 – 1901

It is a fact – or have I dreamt it – that, by means of electricity, the world of matter has become a great nerve, vibrating thousands of miles in a breathless point of time.

– Nathaniel Hawthorne, 1851

Flick a light switch, turn on a television, use a microwave – we take many electrical conveniences for granted. But before the turn of the twentieth century, electricity was just a flickering novelty for most people. Since then, it has become central to our daily lives, a driving force of modern industry, and a multi-billion dollar enterprise. And for people in Edmonton, a home-grown utility has made electricity a reality for more than a century.

EDMONTON'S EARLY GROWTH

Edmonton Electric Lighting and Power Company Limited has its roots in the early history of the City of Edmonton. Like other cities in western Canada, Edmonton began as a fur trading post. After relocating several times, Fort Edmonton was situated in the Edmonton area in 1802, when it was erected on the north bank of the North Saskatchewan River. In 1829, the fort was moved to higher ground near the present location of Alberta's legislature building.

Fort Edmonton experienced two separate waves of newcomers. The first and smaller group were fur traders. These rugged individuals traded with Native peoples at the fort and transported furs along the North Saskatchewan in Edmonton-built York boats.

This way of life was not to continue for long. Demand for furs in North America and Europe diminished. In the 1870s, the rich agricultural land of the West attracted those who saw opportunities for farming and commerce. A new wave of newcomers began to arrive in what is now central Alberta, eager to homestead on the land that had been opened up by the traders.

MILESTONES

1891
Alex Taylor starts the first electric plant in Edmonton.

The C&E Railway between Calgary and South Edmonton is completed.

1892
Edmonton is incorporated as a town.

1895
John Walter's sawmill business is operational in Edmonton.

1896
Marconi applies for a patent on wireless telegraphy.

The Klondike Gold Rush begins.

The first long-distance, high-voltage transmission line (11 kV) carries power from St. Narcisse to Trois-Rivières, Québec, a distance of 29 km.

1898
The Edmonton Golf and Country Club is established.

1899
South Edmonton is incorporated as a town and renamed Strathcona.

The North Saskatchewan River floods Edmonton's river valley.

As businesses were established to provide goods and services for the homesteaders, a town grew up around Fort Edmonton. By 1890, the commercial core of this riverside community was well established along a thoroughfare known as Jasper Avenue *(see map, page 5)*. This main street was lined with two-storey wood-frame stores selling jewelry, shoes, and hardware. There were hotels, a Masonic Hall, and the Hudson's Bay Company store. One general store would later serve as the print shop for Frank Oliver's *Edmonton Bulletin,* one of the city's early newspapers.

The trickle of second-wave settlers became a torrent when the C&E Railway reached the south side of the North Saskatchewan in 1891. Edmonton had been clamouring for a rail line since 1882, when the Canadian Pacific Railway first reached Calgary. Although a railway bridge across the North Saskatchewan to Edmonton would not be built until after the new century began, the future capital benefited from the increasing numbers of settlers arriving at the station on the south side.

Edmonton's population grew steadily. During the summer of 1891, over 300 homesteading entries were filed. In 1892, Edmonton was incorporated as a town. Edmontonians were optimistic that the growth of their community would be sustained. This growing market several hundred kilometres from other major centres, combined with the development of electrical technologies, made a home-grown electrical utility a plausible investment.

THE LIGHTS COME ON IN EDMONTON!

Edmonton had much to offer an electrical utility besides an isolated concentration of consumers. Many of the ingredients necessary for electrical generation were in the community's backyard. The North Saskatchewan was available to supply water to boilers, and the Edmonton area was rich in coal deposits. In fact, many small coal mines operated in the river valley not far from Jasper Avenue.

In 1891, a small group of frontier entrepreneurs recognized how far a local electrical utility could go in Edmonton. In that year, they became the original shareholders of Edmonton Electric Lighting and Power Company Limited. Those who were willing to take that first risk in bringing electricity to Edmonton came from many walks of life. Many names that remain familiar to Edmontonians today appeared in an *Edmonton Bulletin* article about the utility on October 8, 1891. Donald Ross

EDMONTON ELECTRIC LIGHTING AND POWER COMPANY 1902

LEFT: *The board of Edmonton Electric Lighting and Power Company Limited.*

JOHN ALEXANDER McDOUGALL

John A. McDougall's is one of the signatures most often found on early Edmonton Electric Lighting and Power Company records. Elected as the first president of the company, he remained in that position until the utility was sold to the Town of Edmonton in May 1902. John A. McDougall played a leading role in the development of the civic enterprises and businesses of Edmonton.

Originally from Oakwood, Ontario, McDougall first made his way west at 19 years of age by working as a trader and freighter. He first reached Edmonton in 1877, but remained only briefly. He returned from Ontario in 1879 with a new bride, Lovisa. He entered into a business partnership with local businessman Richard Secord; together, they established several of Edmonton's founding businesses.

Their first firm was known as McDougall and Secord; they described themselves as

general merchants, wholesale and retail; buyers and exporters of raw furs; dealers in land scrip and north-west lands; outfitters for survey parties, traders, trappers, miners and others for the north; and suppliers for country stores.

Later, in 1907, this enterprise was sold and the two men set up a financial business that would grow into the $2,500,000 Empire Building.

John A. McDougall's contributions to the Edmonton scene were impressive. He was a charter member of the Edmonton Board of Trade, and chairman of the Edmonton Public School Board. He was also a patron of the arts and benefactor of many welfare and youth organizations. McDougall was a member of the first senate of the University of Alberta. Politically, he was elected mayor of the Town, then City, of Edmonton starting in 1897, and was elected to the legislature in 1909.

McDougall spent the later years of his life travelling throughout the world. He died in Edmonton at the age of 74.

Sources:
The Edmonton Bulletin, *1918,*
The Edmonton Journal, *1963, 1959,*
and City of Edmonton Archives material

owned the Edmonton Hotel. Frank Oliver, a politician and forceful advocate for settler's land rights, operated *The Edmonton Bulletin.* Daniel R. Fraser was the proprietor of a flourmill as well as a sawmill that milled 50,000 feet of lumber daily and employed as many as 70 people. John Walter, operator of a ferry, sawmill, and coal mine, may have supplied his own coal to the power plant. John A. McDougall was elected president of Edmonton Electric Light-

RIGHT: *Looking east down Jasper Avenue in 1896. Signs of innovation, including streetlights and telephone lines, are visible.*

257 JASPER AVENUE EDMONTON LOOKIN EAST

CALIFORNIA RESTAURANT

When the Dominion Telegraph Service line was extended from Hay Lakes to Edmonton in 1879, Alex Taylor came with it as its first operator. He set up an office in John Walter's old log house across the river from Fort Edmonton. That winter, he arranged for weekly news bulletins to be wired to him from Winnipeg. He wrote out these bulletins and left them in Frank Oliver's store, where customers eagerly read them. This, Edmonton's first newspaper, evolved into Frank Oliver's *Edmonton Bulletin*.

Alex Taylor's telegraph operation also led to the telephone business. In 1884, only eight years after Alexander Graham Bell's historic call from Brantford to Paris, Ontario, Alex Taylor encouraged the Dominion Telegraph Service to build a telephone link between his telegraph office and St. Albert, a community a short distance north of Edmonton. This, Alberta's first telephone line, began operation in January 1885. Soon after, Alex established telephone connections between his office and Fort Edmonton, then to various businesses around the community. Edmonton's first telephone system was launched. Alex sold his operation to the City in 1904, and it became the municipally owned Edmonton Telephones.

Alex Taylor was also the Dominion weatherman, postmaster, clerk of the court, and chairman of the public school. In later life, he lost the use of both arms, yet remained active in

serving the community. He set a fine example of dignity and courage.

Adapted from Edmonton: Portrait of a City, *1981*

FIRST POWER PLANT

[FEET RISE IN WATER AUG. 18ᵀᴴ 1899
PUT LIGHTING SYSTEM OUT OF BUSINESS
ND PLANT WAS MOVED TO HIGHER GROUND
NEARER TO OLD FORT

ing and Power Company Limited, and remained in that position until 1902. Alex Taylor, a well-known business owner, was the company's managing director.

On October 23, 1891, Queen Victoria's representative to the North West Territories, Joseph Royal, granted the Edmonton Electric Lighting and Power Company a "letters patent." This gave the fledgling company the right to the "construction, maintenance and operation of works for the production, sale and distribution of electricity for purposes of light, heat and power." As a private company, the capital stock was fixed at $10,000, which was made up of 1,000 shares at $10 each.

LEFT: *Edmonton's power plant as it appeared in the 1890s.*

Under the management of Alex Taylor, Edmonton's power plant was built on the north bank of the North Saskatchewan River, upstream of the Low Level Bridge's present location. This plant had a coal-fired steam boiler and piston-engine-driven generators. Coal, which was stoked by hand, was taken from nearby river valley mines; the river provided easy transportation from mines upstream.

Power poles were installed along Jasper Avenue from 96 Street to 103 Street to power principal buildings and lampposts. Beginning December 22, 1891, electric lights came on in Edmonton. From sunset to 1:00 AM, and in the winter months from 5:30 AM to sunrise, Jasper Avenue was illuminated.

Inroads into Edmonton's market of about 700 citizens (in 1892) came slowly

The basic plan of downtown Edmonton was already formed in 1892. This map shows the location of Edmonton's first power plant (right and below centre) as well as another notable landmark of the day: Fort Edmonton, situated on what is now the grounds of the provincial legislature.

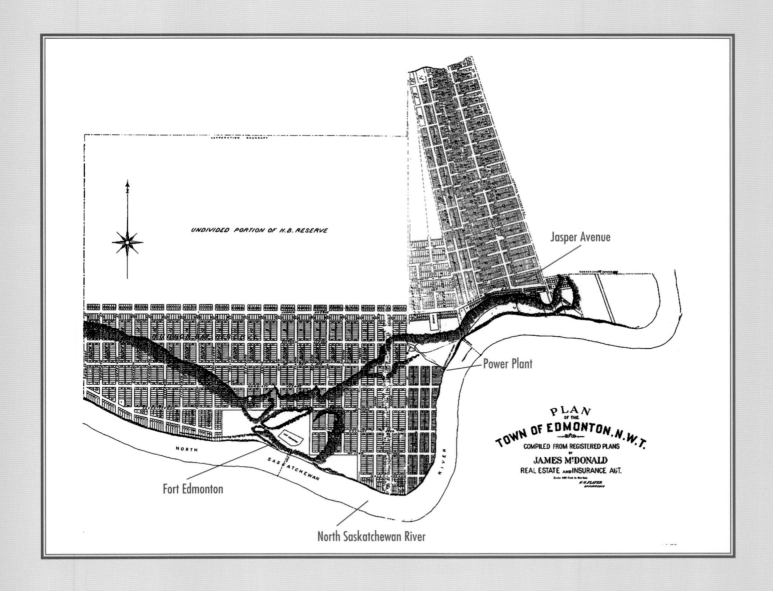

John and Elizabeth Walter

John and Elizabeth Walter formed one of Edmonton's most memorable founding families. John built many of the businesses and institutions that were critical to the city's early development, including a sawmill, a coal mine, and a ferry.

John Walter was born at Senness, on the Orkney Islands, on August 12, 1849. The Hudson's Bay Company lured him to North America; he arrived at York Factory on Hudson Bay in 1870. He then made a long journey to Edmonton, first to Norway House on Lake Winnipeg, then on to Edmonton via the Saskatchewan River. While he could, he travelled by York boat. As winter set in, however, his party continued on by dog train. He finally reached Edmonton on December 24.

Elizabeth Newby was also born in Great Britain, in Yorkshire, in 1860. She came to Canada in 1880, and lived in Toronto for two years. She then travelled by rail to Brandon, and from there made her way to Pheasant Plains by oxcart.

Elizabeth left Pheasant Plains for Winnipeg after only one year; there were too few people of her age living there. After leaving Winnipeg she worked in an orphanage for Native children in Morely. She finally arrived in Edmonton in 1886. There, she met John, whom she married on October 21 of that same year.

By this time, John had become a pillar in the emerging community. He had left the Hudson's Bay Company to pursue his own interests. These interests included Walter's Ferry, the first ferry service to cross the North Saskatchewan, and a boat-building operation that provided small scows to both the Hudson's Bay Company and the government.

When the railway began bringing settlers into the Edmonton area in 1891, John's business diversified. He opened a sawmill, started a coal mine, became the owner of a considerable quantity of land, invested in an electrical generating station, and built a steamer that sailed the North Saskatchewan. He and Elizabeth had two sons: John William and Stanley, who both grew up to operate farms in the Sandy Lake district of Alberta.

A series of floods damaged John's operations around the turn of the century. At this time, many businesses were located on the banks of the river. John urged the government to do something to decrease the severity of the flooding. But a flood in 1915 destroyed not only John's sawmill, but many homes as well. John abandoned his mill, but retained sufficient equity in other interests to go into semi-retirement, though he intended to re-enter the business world.

Unfortunately, however, John died on Christmas morning, 1920, after an operation at Edmonton's Royal Alexandra Hospital. Elizabeth survived her husband, and continued to live in her large green house on the river's edge. Today, Edmonton remembers the Walters through the John Walter Museum.

Source: text prepared by the Northern Alberta Pioneers and Old Timers Association

for Edmonton Electric Lighting and Power. The utility had yet to prove itself: people were not convinced that this new method of lighting was better than the old coal-oil lantern. After all, lanterns required the user to trim wicks and clean chimneys, but once a lantern was lit, it stayed on! This could not always be said for electric lights. Electric generation and distribution were new technologies at the turn of the century, and lacked modern failsafes. Floods and falling trees could cut the electric supply.

According to an original Edmonton Electric Lighting and Power price list of 1891, the cost of lighting a home or business depended on how many lights were wanted.

The rates are as follows: dwelling houses, hotel bedrooms, etc., the first lamp costs $1 a month; two lamps, 85 cents each; more than four lamps, 50 cents each.

The Flood of 1899

The early utility faced a serious challenge in 1899, when the North Saskatchewan rose 41 feet up over the river banks and rolled into the power station. According to Arthur W. Ormsby (later a superintendent of the plant), three to four feet of water had spilled in the building, disabling the operation of the control apparatus and other equipment.

"After we went down McDougall Hill, it was necessary to take a boat to the power plant," said Ormsby in a later interview. The flood caused countless other difficulties that were compounded by a lack of facilities for drying or fixing the wet equipment. As a result, power was off for at least three weeks. It was this disaster, and a smaller flood in 1900,

ARTHUR ORMSBY

Born near Orilla, in Simcoe County, Ontario, Arthur Ormsby gained some experience in telephone operations as a youth. He came to Edmonton on April 16, 1892.

Arthur Ormsby made his first 50 cents in Edmonton repairing a phone in the office of *The Edmonton Bulletin*. Alex Taylor immediately hired him to work as telephone repairman for Taylor's telephone company. At that time, there were between 25 and 30 telephones in Edmonton. Taylor subsequently had Ormsby work at the Electric Lighting and Power Company.

Mr. Ormsby continued to work for the utilities after the Town of Edmonton purchased the electric light and telephone systems. Later, he was employed solely in the electric light department, and eventually became superintendent. In 1919, he was appointed City commissioner, and held the post until 1921, when he entered private business.

Arthur Ormsby was an avid curler. He was one of the 16 people who founded the Edmonton Curling Club in 1892. At that time, the club's "rocks" were kettles filled with sand. "We decided to do it right," Ormsby recalled in an interview he gave in 1961, when he was 92 years old.

So we went to ... the blacksmiths. We described curling rocks to them and they made them from iron blocks. They rounded off the blocks and welded iron handles on them. We ordered just enough rocks for one game at a time.

We sent away to Winnipeg for the dimensions of a curling rink, and marked one out on the river where the Macdonald Hotel is now. We marked the sheet with paint and it lasted all winter.

They used moccasins or skates for shoes, and ordinary household brooms.

We tried curling at night with the light from coal oil lanterns, but it wasn't too successful. Still, we managed to play two or three times a week.

Then, in 1894, the club built a lean-to alongside the lumberyard owned by D.R. Fraser. These facilities attracted the attention of other Alberta teams, and played host to many friendly tournaments.

Sources: The Edmonton Journal, *1954, 1961, and Ormsby's obituary*

that would eventually lead to the decision to move the plant to higher ground.

Once the power plant was back in operation, it remained in good running order under private ownership for several more years. In 1901, however, the company's franchise came to an end. In May 1902, after 10 successful and profitable years under private ownership, Edmonton Electric Lighting and Power Company entered the next phase of its existence, as the first municipally owned electric utility in a Canada, with an installed capacity of 75 kW.

LEFT: *Edmonton's power plant during the disastrous flood of 1899.*

A variety of electrical appliances were available to Edmontonians in this early-twentieth-century store.

CHAPTER 2

Moving with the Times

. . . . .

1902 – 1919

ELECTRICITY: A term applied to that unknown power in nature, which produces electric phenomena.

    – from the 1911
    Handy Electrical Dictionary

The first two decades of the twentieth century brought great change to both Edmonton and the new province of Alberta. The Klondike Gold Rush, begun in 1896, would bring prospectors to the West. Homesteaders continued to flood into the area, attracted by government-funded advertisements promoting settlement. In 1902, a railway bridge was built across the North Saskatchewan River, linking Edmonton to the rest of Canada. Two years later, Edmonton was incorporated as a city. In 1905, it became the capital of the new province of Alberta. By 1908, Edmonton had its own streetcar system. In 1912, Edmonton amalgamated with Strathcona, its neighbour to the south, raising the capital's population from 24,900 to 30,479. By the time an economic slump slowed the city's economy in 1914, Edmonton's population had grown to 72,516.

Edmonton needed to provide many services to its growing population. One of those services was electricity. In 1902, the city became the first in Canada to operate its own electrical utility. To meet the needs of a quadrupling population and increasing per capita demand, the utility increased its generating capacity 13-fold between 1907 and 1914, to 9,375 kW. Those responsible for this expansion faced considerable and unique challenges during this time of growth and transition.

THE SALE OF EDMONTON ELECTRIC LIGHTING AND POWER

Despite the success of Edmonton Electric Lighting and Power under its private owners, there had been occasional lapses in service over the years. The

MILESTONES

1902
The Low Level Bridge connecting Edmonton and Strathcona opens.

1903
The Edmonton Journal begins publication.

1904
The City of Edmonton purchases Alex Taylor's telephone system for $17,000.

1905
Alberta becomes a province within the Dominion of Canada, with Edmonton as its capital city.

1908
Classes begin at the University of Alberta.

Edmonton's streetcar system begins operation.

The City of Edmonton installs the first automatic dialing telephones in North America.

1909
The City of Edmonton hires Alex Decoteau, Canada's first Native police officer. He will later be killed during the Great War.

1911
Alberta's legislature building opens; construction is completed in 1913.

people of Edmonton were voicing their dissatisfaction to Edmonton Town Council. So, in January 1902, when Edmonton Electric Lighting and Power asked for a 10-year renewal of its franchise, the Town decided to purchase the utility outright.

On May 8, 1902 the Town of Edmonton officially took over the ownership of Edmonton Electric Lighting and Power. For $13,500 the municipality acquired the powerhouse, its generators, three boilers, and all other assets.

The electrical utility required considerable renovation when it was transferred to municipal ownership. The generating station had been built on a flood-prone spot on the riverbank. Flooding had caused much as-yet unrepaired damage to equipment and to the foundations under one of the engines; the plant's vulnerability was made clear a short time after the transfer of assets, when a broken crankshaft left the community in total darkness. Town commissioners decided to move the plant out of harm's way. Operations were moved a short distance upstream, to just east of the Walterdale (105 Street) Bridge's present location. The station built at this location was the original Rossdale Power Plant; it included a water pumping station. Coincidentally, the municipal plant was built partly on the site of an early Fort Edmonton.

New equipment was also necessary to make the utility reliable. The generating system in use at the time of transfer of ownership was becoming outdated and, though an existing generator could still be used, more generating capacity was needed.

Considerable funds were spent to build the new building, move in the old equipment, and to purchase and install a new generator. The new facility was named Edmonton Water and Light Station.

The distribution system was also

OPPOSITE: *The Rossdale Power Plant at the turn of the century.* INSET: *The building's datestone survived the demolition of the original plant.*

A REPORT FROM THE PLANT

The [new] electric light plant was installed by the Canadian General Electric Company under the supervision of Chas. L. Leacock ... The old electric light plant, which is in operation as well as the new, consists of two return tubular boilers of 80 horsepower each and one tandem compound engine of 150 horsepower. The boilers are fed by a ... duplex outside packed pump with sufficient capacity to feed four boilers.

The boilers supply steam to run the waterworks pump during the day. Arrangements have lately been made to have the plant fitted with a 1000-horsepower condenser. There is a force of 450 horsepower available for the electric light plant, but only about 250 horsepower are now being used. The pumps require 100 horsepower to run both together. For electric lighting the large engine is run until 11:30 PM, then the 150 horsepower engine until 5:30 PM, when the large engine is run again until morning.

The dynamo and switchboard of the electric light plant were installed by the Canadian General Electric company. The machine is a 3,000 light S.K.C. alternator, excited by a 4 1/2 K.W.D.C. bypolar generator. Upon the blue Vermont marble switchboard are mounted one-volt meters with a new style of double throw switch, which connects either phase of the machine to the motor. There are two ampere meters, one on each circuit, one ground detector; also four switches upon board, one to connect the exciter to the alternator fields, the generator to the bus bars and two switches which connect the bus bars to the transmission line. There are also two rheostats: one controlling the field current of the exciter and the other regulating the amount of current flowing to the alternator field. At the bottom of the switchboards are two regular heads, each one being connected with several coils of armature, allowing an adjustment of voltage if either phase is more heavily loaded than the other.

Provision is also made for running the old machine at the same time as the new one. A lamp mounted upon the switches indicates by its pulsations the relative speeds of the two machines: when the lamp is bright the two generators are in phase and the switches can be closed, paralleling the same.

From The Daily Edmonton, *1903*

Note: Generation at this time was two-phase alternating current. Three-phase alternating current later became standard.

ALBERTA BECOMES A PROVINCE

Inauguration Day, September 1, 1905
Those were wonderful days, the days surrounding September 1, 1905. They were wonderful nights, too. In fact, it might be said the nights were almost more wonderful than the days ... During the nights Edmonton, the new capital, rivaled Paris for the title: City of Light. Edmonton blazed with lights as it never had before. And the electric light department of the new capital helped to make it so, by giving everyone [two days] of free power ... It was on the "powerhouse." Let Edmonton be the city of light. The first place they decorated was Alberta College, just off First and Jasper. Alberta College was headquarters for the inauguration revelry, and string after string of coloured lights were hung on the college. Down on 98th Street the front of the fire hall was ablaze with mottoes and designs, worked out in coloured lights.

Across from the fire hall on Jasper Avenue, the round tower of the Alberta Hotel was transformed into a barber pole by alternate strings of red, white, and blue lights. [Along] the length of Jasper Avenue ... up to Fourth Street – there were arches proclaiming the greatness of the new province. The arches were hung with sheaves of wheat, evergreens, and of course, lights. The Hudson's Bay store and Revillon Freres were spangled with white stars. The residential streets were bright with Japanese lanterns hung in the trees. The very night was dazzled by the brightness. ... By night Edmonton was a veritable beacon ....

From The Edmonton Story,
by Tony Cashman, *1956*

MILESTONES
(continued)

1911
Calgary Power Company Limited is registered.

1912
Strathcona amalgamates with Edmonton.

1913
The High Level and Walterdale bridges are opened in Edmonton.

The Alberta legislature building opens.

The City of Edmonton appoints Annie Jackson, Canada's first female police officer.

1914
World War 1 begins.

1915
Edmonton's Commercial Grads basketball club is formed.

Edmonton's 49th Battalion goes overseas to fight in Europe.

1916
Alberta women gain the right to vote in provincial elections.

Prohibition comes to Alberta.

1918
The Spanish influenza epidemic strikes Alberta.

Peter McNaughton

According to an *Edmonton Bulletin* article dating from June 5, 1916, Peter McNaughton was "one of the best-known Edmonton citizens." He was a graduate of the mechanical engineering program at McGill University, and a member of the Canadian Society of Mechanical Engineers. McNaughton apparently came to Edmonton from Huntingdon, Quebec in 1898, and was soon employed as the power engineer at the city power plant. He retained this position until 1910.

McNaughton was active in civic affairs, and spent a two-year term as a City commissioner. He earned the esteem and confidence of a great many people. In a September 1903 letter to the Town of Edmonton, for example, he makes a request to the council for holidays on behalf of power plant employees. No doubt his workers respected him. "Of a genial disposition, he was exceedingly well

liked by all. A mechanic, a scientist, a soldier, he was a typical type of the all-round Canadian."

McNaughton had always taken an interest in military affairs, and therefore was eager to sign up for service soon after World War I broke out. Like so many others, he was never to return. Sometime in June, 1916 his wife was notified that machine gunner Peter McNaughton had been killed in action.

Source: The Edmonton Bulletin, *1916*

improved and expanded; new poles were installed while existing ones were altered for better transmission. In addition, a newly installed series street lighting system meant that streetlights could be turned on from a single point; previously, each one had to be turned on individually. This was fortunate, as the streetlights were growing in number: there were only 53 lights in 1905, and 1,550 by 1920.

Before the Town of Edmonton took over the provision of electricity to its residents, the service was provided only until late in the evening. With municipal ownership, service was increased to 24 hours a day.

A Growing Market

Despite the purchase of new equipment, demand for power soon exceeded the utility's generating capacity. The area of the city grew from 7.17 square miles in 1904 to 14.67 square miles in 1908 and to 40.88 square miles in 1914. Furthermore, the population increased from 14,088 in 1906 to 23,000 in 1909, then to 72,516 by 1914. In 1908, the City had also taken over ownership of the street railway system, which operated on direct current electricity. Grain milling, grain elevators, machine shops, and packing plants established themselves in Edmonton. Expansion of the power and light service would have to keep step

with the general development of the city.

From 1904 to 1914, Edmonton undertook yearly expansions of electrical services. Two million dollars was raised for the power plant, and $1 million dollars was raised for the distribution system. These investments soon began to pay off; by the end of this period, the utility was producing a $300,000 surplus for the City every year.

How was the money spent? Additions were made to the Rossdale building in 1906 and 1908. In 1908, a Loomis-Pettibone gas producer of 750-horse-power capacity was installed, along with a gas-engine-driven three-phase alternator. Then, in 1910, a 2,000-kW turbo-generator was installed. Two more generators were added in the following year: a second 2,000-kW unit, and a 400-kW direct current generator that energized the street railway. The railway required more power, however, so an additional 750-kW direct current generator was added in 1912. Then again in 1913, a 4,000-kW turbo-generator was purchased and installed to bring the total alternating current generating capacity at Rossdale to 9,375 kW.

The distribution system, too, was in dire need of renovation; it had become a system of feeders so complicated that economical operation became impossible. With the economic depression during World War I, however, there was little that could be done to improve the system until 1922.

Beyond City Borders

From time to time, as the city's power plant was stretched to the limit, alternatives to the utility's thermal generators were examined. In 1904, at the suggestion of the Edmonton Board of Trade, a

TOP LEFT and **RIGHT:** *Additions were made to the Rossdale Power Plant in 1906 and 1908.*

RIGHT: *Streetcars running on direct current power were an important part of Edmonton's transport system in 1910.*

BELOW RIGHT: *Both the legislature and the High Level Bridge were under construction in 1912. Rossdale is visible on the far right of this photograph.*

COAL!

Edmonton's first electric generating units were fed steam produced in coal-fired boilers. The Town of Edmonton contracted Samuel Moran to provide this coal. Moran was to provide graded coal to the generating station for a flat fee of $225 per month. The contract obliged Moran to supply fuel sufficient to supply 1,500 customers. If the customer base increased, Moran would receive an additional $15 for every 100 customers in excess of 1,500.

In accordance with the policy of the Commissioners, the management of the substation was taken over by the Power Plant from May 1st, 1913, and at the same time debenture liabilities amounting to $149,551.03 were transferred from the Street Railway books to those of the Power Plant. At this time the only substation was a small wooden structure on Syndicate Avenue [95 Street], equipped with one 500 K.W. motor generator. As it was decided to abandon this site, plans were at once prepared and construction commenced on a permanent brick substation of

modern type, situated on John Street [80 Street], adjoining the new car barns. A transmission voltage of 6,600 volts was determined to be the most economical, and was, therefore, adopted – two 1,000 K.V.A. three phase, step-down transformers being installed in the substation. During November, 1913, the new substation was put into service with one 500 K.W. motor generator, which was transferred from a temporary location at the Power Plant. Early in 1914 the old substation will be dismantled and the motor generator and equipment re-erected in the new one, which will then contain 1,000 K.W. rating of synchronous motor-generating machinery and 2,000 K.V.A. transformer capacity.

*From the Edmonton Light and Power
1913 Annual Report*

LEFT: *100 Substation in 2000.*

HOW DID ROSSDALE GET ITS NAME?

Rossdale, or Ross Flats as it was first known, got its name from local hotelier Donald Ross. Ross came to Edmonton in the early 1870s, where he was to erect the third house built in Edmonton, after the Hudson's Bay Company and the Mission. Being one of the few European men in town, his hospitality was stretched to the limit; thus, he decided to charge visitors $0.50 for meals. This was his start as a hotelier. He opened the Edmonton Hotel in 1876. Ross's hotel was the first to be established west of Portage La Prairie. Fitted up with rooms, kitchen, bar, and billiard tables, the Edmonton Hotel would remain as a landmark until 1925, when it was destroyed by fire. No doubt the Edmonton Hotel was one of Edmonton Light and Power's preferred customers. The power plant, still situated in Rossdale, continues to bear Donald Ross's name.

Sources: The Edmonton Bulletin *1915,* The Edmonton Journal *1955,* The Alberta Hotelman *1965, and City of Edmonton Archive material*

consultant was hired to examine the possibility of a hydro-electric plant on the North Saskatchewan River 50 miles to the west of the city. According to the report finally made available in 1907, this was a feasible plan, though quite expensive: it required a capital outlay of $1 million and yearly costs of $139,000.

So the hydro-electric idea was shelved until 1910, when the City explored the possibility of a hydro-electric facility on the Athabasca River, at Grand Rapids, 200 miles north of the city. This idea was soundly defeated at the polls. Again, in 1912, the idea of a hydro plant on the Saskatchewan was investigated but later rejected. Though the City wanted to deal with its growing need for power, it

THE BOUILLON AFFAIR: THE POWER PLANT CONNECTION

Politics are a part of business at municipally owned utilities like Edmonton Light and Power. The "Bouillon Affair" of 1911 made this particularly apparent.

Mr. Bouillon moved from Seattle to Edmonton in April 1910. The City hired him to manage its municipal utilities; as a commissioner, Bouillon was paid the then-astronomical figure of $10,000 per year. This high salary didn't please everyone, and so Mr. Bouillon began his career in Edmonton on the wrong foot. This was just the beginning. As time went by, Bouillon proved to be what people called a "czar," about as close as one could get to a dictator: he wanted to run all the departments himself and in his own way. City aldermen attempted to get rid of Bouillon after realizing that he did not meet expectations. This task involved legal and civic battles, and spurred a media war that produced both comedy and drama for local citizens.

In early January of 1911, eight days after the public declaration of war between Bouillon and some of the City aldermen, Commissioner Bouillon refused to recommend that the city power plant superintendent go along with a civic party to eastern Canada on a buying trip. Two days later he fired both the power plant superintendent and the head of the street railway. He refused to give any reasons. When councillors protested, he reminded them that hiring and firing was a power given to commissioners. This further enraged the councillors, and they "fixed" him by refusing to allow him to go on a three-week holiday. The street railway also sent him a bill for $22.50 for four late streetcars he had ordered to run after midnight mass on Christmas Eve.

Later that year, Edmonton City Council decided to have Bouillon hire an engineer to advise it on big purchases like power plant equipment. Bouillon hired a fellow who initially seemed competent. But it was soon discovered that his main engineering experience had been gained while installing some minor equipment at the Ponoka Mental Hospital.

Finally, after numerous legal challenges, the City was able to rid itself of Bouillon: he was fired. Ironically, he went back to Seattle where he took a job managing a big shipyard – for a salary of $40,000 per year.

seemed unable to settle on a solution. Finally, in 1914, it appeared as though the City had resolved to purchase new equipment, including a boiler system, for Rossdale. Despite these intentions, this initiative was delayed when World War 1 broke out.

AMALGAMATION

When Edmonton amalgamated with Strathcona in 1912, the Strathcona Power Plant became Edmonton's responsibility. Edmonton had occasionally purchased power from this plant to meet peak demands. Large sums of money had been spent on machinery prior to the amalgamation. According to the Power House Annual Report of 1913, two boilers, together with a 600-kW slow-speed engine and alternator, had been put into service in Strathcona. A new brick stack had been built and a considerable amount of money spent on coal unloading facilities. Unfortunately, after amalgamation the City operated this plant only when it was necessary, and it contributed only 1.66% of the total output in 1913. The poor condition of the building and its foundations, as well as the high cost of fuel, made the plant uneconomical to operate.

ALLIANCE POWER COMPANY

Ownership of utilities was a hotly debated topic in the early decades of the twentieth century – many thought that public utilities should be privatized, while others were opposed to this idea.

Edmonton Light and Power did not escape scrutiny. City Council had received numerous proposals from private businesses that wanted to participate in the electrical industry. When the question was put to the public in a referendum, voters agreed that this would be a positive step forward. Consequently, proposals were called for, and from 1916 to 1919 the Alliance Power Company took over the power plant. It sold power in bulk to the Electric Light and Power Department of the City of Edmonton. This arrangement came to an end due to financial difficulties.

Undoubtedly, the City of Edmonton faced many challenges as it kept up with the ever-increasing demand for electrici-

ELECTRIC SIGNS ARE BEING DISCARDED

"Illuminated electric signs as a method of advertising will soon be a thing of the past," said Electric Superintendent Ormsby to the *Bulletin* yesterday, in discussing this method of street advertising.

"Montreal, Toronto, Vancouver, Winnipeg and all the other large cities are drawing the lines tighter on electric sign advertising, and in Minneapolis and St. Paul, where it used to be a big feature, it is being rapidly discarded," he continued.

"What is the objection?" the *Bulletin* representative asked.

"The great complaint is the unsightly appearance of the signs in day time. They resemble rookeries in the best parts of the city," replied Mr. Ormsby.

"Another reason is that it is hard to regulate them. Every person who gets a sign tries to go one better than his neighbour, and completely eclipse him if he can. You can see that already along Jasper Avenue.

"Edmonton will give more attention to street lighting, as Minneapolis and St. Paul are now doing, and the result will be a much better appearance both in the day and at night."

from The Edmonton Bulletin, *1910*

POWER PLANT AND PUMPING STATION WITHSTOOD TEST: *Flats Flooded to First Street*

At the power plant, the scene was rather remarkable. The entire staff is working under high pressure, and in some instances, under high water. Several of the [ash] pits [in the plant's basement] have from four to six feet of water in them. As the power plant is the vital heart of the city, Mayor Henry and Commissioner Harlson kept gravitating to this point to see how things were going. The water kept rising in the pits at the average rate of one foot every hour. But it was noticed that by three o'clock in the afternoon the rate of rise was decreasing and it was felt that unless the entire plant was flooded in from the surrounding land, it would be possible to keep it going.

The only way in which it was possible to keep the plant running was to keep ... the water out of the ash pits. Here a big six-inch hose was attached to a high power pump and a great stream of water was forced out of the pits just a trifle faster than it was coming in from the river. In this way the water was kept below the level of the fireboxes and steam was kept up, although the stokers were working in water all day long to do it.

from The Edmonton Bulletin, *1915*

ty during the period from 1902 to 1914. However, financial records show that the City made a considerable profit from the utility during this time, and was able to keep rates among the lowest in Canada, at $0.08 per kWh.

Over the same period, from 1902 to 1914, the ability of the power plant to meet demand also increased. From a net capacity of 225 kW in 1902 (after the upgrade), net capacity had risen to 9,375 kW by 1914.

When the Great War came to a close in 1918, soldiers began to return to Edmonton. Businesses again began to flourish. Edmonton Light and Power would continue to face the challenge of responding to a growing demand for power in a thriving city.

ABOVE: *The accounting office at Rossdale early in the twentieth century.*

CHAPTER 3

Expanding Power

. . . . .

1920 – 1929

On May 1, 1922, Alberta's first commercial radio station, CJCA, went on the air in Edmonton. The 50-W station was located in the offices of *The Edmonton Journal*. At the time, there were 200 radios in the city. By 1927, 10,000 licensed radio sets were in use in Alberta. For the first time, Albertans in isolated parts of the province could hear news, weather, and entertainment programs. They could also learn about the lives and interests of other people in the province.

During the 1920s, the applications of electricity greatly diversified. While radio was enabling people to learn about the wider world, other electrical appliances were transforming people's domestic lives. In Edmonton and Calgary, electric wringer washers replaced washboards, and brooms were sacrificed to the vacuum cleaner. Kerosene lamps were relegated to

BELOW: *A growing number of customers took advantage of a variety of electrical conveniences in the 1920s.*

MILESTONES

1923
Natural gas is first used for domestic purposes in Edmonton.

CKCK Regina makes Canada's first radio broadcast of a hockey game.

1924
Oil is struck in Turner Valley, southwest of Calgary.

1926
Blatchford Field, Canada's first municipal airport, is established in Edmonton.

1927
Canada celebrates its sixtieth anniversary as a nation.

Canadian Utilities begins generating electricity for small Alberta communities.

1928
The City of Edmonton installs one of the world's largest 10,000-kW turbine generators at its Rossdale plant.

1929
Alberta pilots Wilfred "Wop" May and Vic Horner fly desperately needed diphtheria antitoxin to Fort Vermilion.

Emily Murphy and Nellie McClung succeed in having British courts declare that Canadian women are legally "persons."

CITY LIGHT & POWER DEPARTMENT
1926
17,333 Customers SERVICE 1905
650 Customers

Obsolete technology and massive demand increases posed just a few of the challenges that faced Edmonton's electrical utility during the 1920s. Fortunately, an able manager was available to guide the Rossdale Power Plant through this tumultuous period. William J. Cunningham, a soft-spoken man with a strong English accent, was born in Altrincham, England in 1886. He studied engineering at the University of Manchester, and eventually moved to North America to work for the City power plant in Calgary. By 1915, he was assistant superintendent of the plant.

Later, Cunningham left his job to join the war effort. His skills were valuable to the Royal Gun Factory in Woolwich, England, where he worked as a munitions inspector. After the war, Cunningham returned to Calgary and resumed his work at the power plant. In 1919, however, Cunningham accepted a job as the superintendent of Edmonton's power plant. Cunningham's job in Edmonton would expand twice over the following few years: in 1920, he was made responsible for the water plant, and in 1925, he was asked to manage the city's electric railway system.

Cunningham was intimately concerned with the day-to-day work of the areas he managed. He kept himself informed of the latest innovations in engineering technology. In 1927, he travelled to England to visit other power plants and learn about innovations in electrical technology. During his tenure at the Edmonton power plant, Cunningham used his knowl-

edge and credibility to advise city politicians on costly expansions as well as collaborations with other companies.

Like many Rossdale managers before and since, Cunningham was active in many voluntary associations in Edmonton. He was president of the Association of Professional Engineers of Alberta and of the Edmonton Golf and Country Club; he was also a member of the Masonic Lodge.

Unfortunately, all of this activity, coupled with hard work and heavy responsibilities, may have cost Cunningham his health. In 1934 he suffered a major stroke and died at 47 years of age. His death shocked city officials. According to an account in the May 14, 1937 issue of *The Edmonton Bulletin,*

> *[Cunningham] was highly regarded by civic officials with whom he worked and also by the large staff of employees of both the power and street railway departments for his fairness, good nature, and unceasing efforts to better conditions in the branch of industry in which he attained such a high place.*

Sources: The Edmonton Journal, *1934, 1935, 1937;* Edmonton Bulletin, *1934*

LEFT: *William Cunningham.*

BELOW: *Chain grate stokers used with a boiler installed in 1914. Cunningham is in the right foreground wearing a white shirt and tie.*

garden sheds and electric light bulbs hung from the ceilings of many urban homes. This trend toward greater consumption, coupled with a growing population, meant explosive increases in demand for electricity.

MANAGEMENT AT THE UTILITIES

William Cunningham was the superintendent of Rossdale Power Plant in the 1920s. Although Rossdale was managed separately from the electrical distribution system (which was called the Electric Light and Power Department, and managed by superintendents Barnhouse and Murphy) during this time, many other aspects of the city's infrastructure came under Cunningham's wing. In 1920, Cunningham began to manage the water treatment and pumping plant. This was a logical arrangement, as the power plant provided the electric energy and steam necessary for the operation of the pumps, filters, and other equipment that the pumping and filtration systems needed. The power plant also provided warm water to keep the treatment plants, filters, and the distribution mains operational in cold weather. The power plant supplied direct current electricity to the street railway; thus, Cunningham came to manage the streetcar system as well.

A GROWING DEMAND

Between 1920 and 1929, Edmonton's population grew from 61,045 to 74,298.

One of the reasons for this growth was the number of soldiers returning from the battlefields of World War I. It was a time of relief and optimism following the harsh days of war; thus, new industries were established and both factories and homes were built. Construction boomed, more than doubling in the latter half of the decade.

According to a table that appeared in *The Edmonton Journal* in 1935, Edmonton's Electric Light and Power Department had 15,445 electricity customers in January 1921. By January 1930, this number had increased to 20,082. The demand for electricity in the same period rose from 1,266,900 kWh for January 1921 to 3,515,163 kWh for the same month in 1930.

The power plant required expansion due to increased demand and the need for greater reliability. Electricity was no longer just a convenience or a luxury by the 1920s: it had become a necessity. Superintendent Cunningham recognized this fact:

The supply of energy must not fail for one second – the lighting of the homes, hospitals, public buildings, and streets are dependent upon it. The wheels of industry must be kept turning by the manifold applications of the electric motor, and transportation provided by the energy supplied to the street railway lines. In case of trouble arising in the complicated structure of producing and delivering energy, the first aim of the staff is to maintain and restore the service, no matter what the cost.

NEW EQUIPMENT NEEDED

Between 1914 and 1921, the generating capacity of the Rossdale Power Plant did not expand. As demand increased during this time, more pressure was placed on rapidly aging equipment. In 1920, machinery breakdowns, overhauls, and repair work cost the city a staggering $56,865. As Superintendent Cunningham noted:

Probably owing to the fact that the first period of growth occurred during the years in which rapid development was taking place in the design of electrical machinery, a large amount of equipment was installed which quickly became obsolete.

Throughout the 1920s, the city would invest in new and innovative equipment

that would expand the installed generating capacity of the Rossdale Power Plant to 23,000 kW. A 5,000-kW General Electric-Curtis turbo-generator with a Wheeler condensing plant was installed in 1921. To accommodate this equipment, the basement floor of the power plant was excavated and a new foundation built. The leaky roof over the engine room was replaced, and a transformer and switching station were built.

In 1922, old and dangerous switching control equipment was also replaced. New circuit breakers, bus-bar equipment, and three new transformers were installed. In the end, Rossdale's entire output was operated by remote control from the board located in the turbine room.

The greatest source of pride for staff at the power plant during the 1920s was the 10,000-kW Parsons turbine generator that operated at a speed of 3,600 RPM. Installed in 1927, this piece of equipment represented a major technological advance. Previous machines were smaller

or ran at lower speeds. The new high-speed generator was the first of its type installed in North America. It cost the city $215,000. It demonstrated the progressive, courageous attitude of the City and the utility. Sir Charles A. Parsons and Lady Parsons travelled to Edmonton from Newcastle-upon-Tyne, England, to commission the unit in 1929.

DISTRIBUTION

The effective distribution of electricity was also a priority for Edmonton's power managers in the 1920s. Bus bars, feeders, and transformers were updated. In 1922, a 13,200-V ring main feeder system was started. Many new substations were built. Substations were distribution centres where voltage was reduced from 13,200-V to 2,300-V. This lower level of voltage was carried down streets and lanes and converted to 110-V for use in the homes of residential customers. According to Electric Light and Power Superintendent Barnhouse, substations made it possible for linemen to

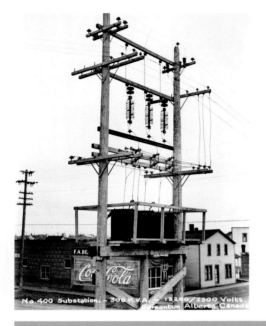

No. 400 Substation. - 300 K.V.A. - 13200/2200 Volts. Edmonton, Alberta, Canada

Standard 50-ft. pole. Common construction. High Tension Feeder, Primary Light and Power Secondary, Street Lighting, Telephone, etc.

FAR LEFT: *400 Substation in the 1920s.*

LEFT: *Fifty-foot poles were erected across Edmonton to carry telephone, power, and street railway lines.*

A Memorable Machine

The 10,000-kW Parsons turbine generator that was installed in Rossdale with so much pride in 1927 was sold to Saskatchewan Power in 1950. The Saskatchewan utility did not take with it the Howden exciter and steam engine (LEFT) that had worked with the generator. It was therefore decided to place the exciter on a small pedestal between the sundial and the flagpole which were then in front of the Rossdale office. Unfortunately, politicians raised concerns about this arrangement and the machine was sold for scrap.

make repairs to the distribution network in one part of the city without shutting down the main power line.

The Street Railway

Edmonton's power plant provided electricity to the electric streetcars that rumbled along the city's main arteries. The production of direct current for the street railway posed special problems. In the early 1920s, motor generators at 100 Substation (located at 80 Street and 115 Avenue) produced 1,200 kW for the railway. Generators at the Rossdale Power Plant produced an additional 2,200 kW for the service. Since power was supplied from these two centres only, the drop in voltage was excessive at various points on the streetcar system, making it difficult for the cars to start moving again after dropping off passengers. The problem was made worse by

the demand for power, which increased as the railway system expanded.

With the return of the soldiers following World War 1, ridership on the brown and yellow electric streetcars increased steadily. Railway lines were extended and more streetcars were purchased. The aging equipment at the power plant and motor generators at 100 Substation could not keep pace with this increase. Equipment breakdowns meant that rail service was interrupted for days at a stretch; in one case, a short circuit in one of the motor generators took four days to repair.

In March 1927, Superintendent Cunningham put in an urgent request to City commissioners recommending that a second-hand 750-kW motor generator be purchased from the City of Calgary, to be used to provide electricity for the street railway. The request was granted. The purchase cost $17,000, including dismantling, freight, and installation of the unit.

In 1929, a mercury arc power rectifier was purchased to convert alternating current to direct current for the street railway. This increased the supply of current available to the railway system by making the total output of Rossdale eligible for powering streetcars.

In the long term, Cunningham proposed building additional substations and replacing outdated equipment to effectively deal with the streetcar problem. While City commissioners embraced Cunningham's proposals, the Great Depression of the 1930s would delay the implementation of many of them. Provision of power to the street railway would continue to be a technically demanding and financially draining problem for superintendents and City commissioners alike for many years to come.

THE TROUBLE MAN

The proliferation of electrical appliances in the 1920s may have made life easier for consumers, but it also meant that more things could go wrong. In the early 1920s, a customer who noticed a strange burning smell coming from an electric wringer washer might call the

RIGHT: *Early mercury arc rectifiers such as these were used to convert alternating current into direct current to power the street railway.*

COAL AND ASH

Rossdale Power Plant frequently turned to new generating equipment to increase efficiency and output. However, there were other ways to meet production goals. A more efficient and reliable coal-handling system was one. A new coal crusher was purchased and installed in December 1920. Mechanical coal stokers to feed several of the boilers were added in 1922. Boiler-induced draft fans were also installed. These additions improved efficiency so effectively that boilers installed in 1914 were able to function until 1931.

Steps were also taken to improve the plant's ash disposal system. In 1921, a light industrial track with dump cars was installed in the basement of the plant. These cars removed ashes and dumped them into an underground bunker. A locomotive crane removed the ashes from the bunker and loaded

them into railway cars.

The disposal system modifications were successful: in 1922, 18 men were needed to remove the ash. A year later, only 8 men were required.

BELOW: *Stokers at Rossdale in 1923.*

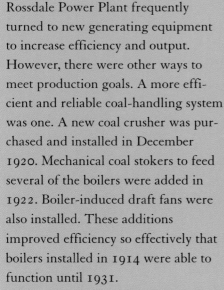

Electric Lighting and Power Department's "trouble man." He would appear on the customer's doorstep, attempt to find the source of the problem, and fix it.

The trouble man was on duty until midnight every day except Saturday and Sunday. On those nights, the trouble phone was switched to 100 Substation so the substation operator could respond to calls. By 1926, this arrangement was no longer practical.

In a December 6, 1926 letter to City Commissioner Mitchell, Electric Light and Power Superintendent Murphy asks that trouble service be extended to include the weekends:

THE FIRST NEON SIGNS

Neon signs were first installed along Calgary's Eighth Avenue and Edmonton's Jasper Avenue in 1928. Though signs lit with incandescent bulbs were common, neon was an entirely new and enchanting way to advertise, and quickly gained popularity.

Advertisements urged merchants to write their messages "in letters of fire – Neon." At first, the signs were available only in red – the colour naturally emitted when electricity passes through neon gas. The lettering on the Darling's Drug Store sign installed at the corner of Jasper Avenue and 102 Street in December, 1928 owed its crimson colour to neon gas. There was truth to claims that neon made "indelible impressions" on the minds of customers, because many Edmonton residents still remember the Darling's Drug Store sign.

Adapted from The Spirit of Alberta: An Illustrated Heritage, *by Helen LaRose*

As an example of the necessity for this arrangement, we might refer to the case of trouble that occurred in the north end district about a week ago ... The office trouble man went off duty at 7 PM and phone calls were switched to the substation; as the substation operator was then busy testing switches, etc., it was not possible for him to give proper attention to the many phone calls received.

Mitchell agreed to Murphy's request. Later that month, weekend trouble service was established, with the "trouble man" receiving $4.00 for each six-hour weekend shift.

LIGHTING UP THE STREETS

Traffic jams were becoming common in Edmonton by 1927, as there were between 7,000 and 8,000 cars in the city. "Tin Lizzies" – Model T Fords – vied for parking spots in Edmonton's market square (now Churchill Square). Trucks

BELOW: *Edmonton's electricity generating station as it appeared in the early 1920s.*

replaced horse-drawn delivery wagons. As the number of automobiles grew, so did the need for improved street lighting. Edmonton's Electric Light and Power Department responded by increasing the number of streetlights to 2,016.

A PROFITABLE VENTURE

Even with a large number of equipment purchases, the City's electric utilities were able to maintain healthy surpluses throughout the 1920s. In 1928, Edmonton's Electric Lighting and Power Department showed a surplus of $1,593,433. That same year, the Power and Pumping Plant had a surplus of $1,186,039. The benefits of these surpluses were passed on to customers in the form of lowered rates. The basic rate for electricity in the 1920s hovered between $0.07 and $0.08 per kWh, with the average customer paying between $4.46 and $5.10 per month for electricity.

Attracted by the healthy balance sheets, Canadian Utilities offered to purchase

Private vs. Public

Albertans have long debated the merits of public ownership of their municipal electric utilities. A pamphlet entitled "Opposition to Public Operation" circulated in Edmonton in the 1920s, promoting the benefits of private ownership of utilities. It argued that "men who are competent to run great enterprises are not in politics, and if they are hired to run municipal utilities they are too much hindered by politics."

It seems that many Albertans agreed. Small private companies generated power for many of Alberta's communities in the early years of electricity. Except for a brief period in its history, Edmonton was the exception to this rule. While operation of the utility would at times be "hindered" by politics, Edmonton would eventually have the largest public power system in Alberta. In contrast, Calgary Power, Canadian Utilities, and Northland Utilities would buy out most of the local power plants in other parts of the province.

BELOW: *In the 1920s, Albertans were subjected to persuasive advertising that argued for privately owned utilities.*

To Make a Kilowatt-hour

Municipal plants use this much fuel and labor } While { companies use this much fuel and labor

Municipal plants, according to the United States census, use nearly three (2.7) times as much fuel and labor as companies do to produce one kilowatt-hour

Edmonton's electric system in 1928. In a report that year, Superintendent Cunningham explored the advantages and disadvantages of a sale. Cunningham pointed out that selling the utility would remove the immediate necessity of buying much-needed new equipment and expanding Rossdale Power Plant. However, all investments in the utility were quickly recouped through increased sales of electrical power.

The offers to purchase Edmonton's electric light and power system were quickly rejected. As Commissioner Mitchell stated:

> *The fact that today certain powerful private interests are knocking at the door to be heard in support of their proposals to undertake the operation of some of these utilities on supposedly advantageous terms, merely goes to prove that they recognize the value of the City's utilities as a large field of industrial development which, with its promising future, warrants a considerable investment of capital in acquiring these utilities.*

Attention – Citizens of Edmonton!

Although the City refused to sell its power utility to a private firm, it did not close the door to all collaborations with private enterprise. A memo dated December 28, 1928 provides the earliest evidence that such a collaboration was under consideration. In this memo, Power Plant Superintendent Cunningham briefly explores the implications of a possible interconnection of Edmonton's electrical supply with the system operated by Calgary Power Ltd.

On March 11, 1929, Calgary Power

Ltd. submitted a proposal to sell secondary power to, and interchange power with, the Rossdale Power Plant. In an August 23, 1929 report exploring the implications of such a relationship, Cunningham states that the existing equipment at Edmonton's power plant could not be expected to meet the growing peak-load demands projected for the winter of 1930–1931.

According to Cunningham, Edmonton had two options: it could build a new extension to the Rossdale Power Plant, which meant purchasing efficient but expensive machinery. Or, it could enter into a mutually advantageous relationship with Calgary Power in which resources would be pooled. Cunningham believed that Calgary Power's offer looked good in theory, but knew that, in practice, it would require extreme care to ensure efficiency and low power costs. It would also only delay the need to purchase equipment; Edmonton would still need to replace machines that were rapidly becoming obsolete.

Cunningham knew that Calgary Power was developing a province-wide system of generation and transmission. By providing industries with competitive rates for power, the company was also attracting many large manufacturing businesses to Calgary. Manitoba Steel and Iron and the Dominion Bridge Company Ltd. had both located in Calgary because of lower energy costs. In Cunningham's view, if Edmonton and Calgary were receiving their electrical energy from a common system, this difference would be removed and the

RIGHT: *Inside the Rossdale plant in the 1920s. The tallest unit is the 750-kW triple expansion and engine, installed in 1910 and removed in 1949.*

playing field would be more level.

Not all of Edmonton's citizens were enthusiastic about the possibility of their publicly owned utility entering into a relationship with a privately owned company. In at least one case, flyers were distributed and a public meeting held to protest the interchange with Calgary Power. One handbill read:

Attention – Citizens of Edmonton! The aldermen are PLEDGED to PUBLIC OWNERSHIP. Without any mandate from the people they now intend to enter into an agreement with Calgary Power Company. The agreement is in effect a FRANCHISE. It is an attack on PUBLIC OWNERSHIP! THE THIN EDGE OF THE WEDGE! At its termination Edmonton will be at the mercy of Calgary Power Company. CALGARY POWER COMPANY IS NOT TO DELIVER POWER TO THE CITY UNTIL

THE SUMMER OF 1930. There is plenty of time to ascertain the wishes of the citizens. LET THEM DECIDE! The contract IS NOT favorable to Edmonton. Calgary Power will not bring industries to Edmonton. The motto of the Council should be EDMONTON FIRST! Attend the public meeting at the Memorial Hall on Thursday, September the 12th at 8:00 p.m.

Despite these protests, Edmonton City Council accepted a modified version of Calgary Power's offer. Thus began a relationship that would provide ongoing challenges for the managers of both utilities for many years.

BUILDING FOR THE FUTURE

Besides agreeing to collaborate with Calgary Power, the City adopted an earlier plan by Cunningham. This, an ambitious five-year proposal to improve the power plant, consisted of building an

extension to the existing plant, erecting new buildings, acquiring and installing new equipment, and disposing of old machinery.

Cunningham pointed out that the costs of these improvements should not concern the City of Edmonton:

Provided the requirements warrant the expenditure, and the economic results attained absorb the increased charges, the amount of the investment is a secondary consideration. The City of Edmonton is actually only lending its credit for an investment which will produce large returns. This utility has not cost the citizens of Edmonton one dollar, and by a further extension of credit, the result will be decreased charges for light and power than exist at the present time.

Cunningham could not foresee the economic crisis that would soon blanket the world. The Wall Street crash and subsequent economic downturn would curtail some of the utility's ambitious expansion plans, but not for long. In 1930, the City of Edmonton would approve the first phase of Cunningham's proposal, and invest scarce dollars on expanding the Rossdale Power Plant to meet the need for electricity.

ABOVE: *In the second decade of the twentieth century, Edmonton's Electric Light and Power Department had its offices at 242 MacDougall Avenue. The people in this photograph may have staffed the early utility.*

CHAPTER 4

Growth Despite Hard Times

. . . . .

1930 – 1939

On October 24, 1929, an event occurred that would change the lives of people around the world for the next decade. On that day, so many people lost so much money on the New York Stock Exchange that the world economy was thrown into what is now known as the Great Depression. Despite this, Edmonton Light and Power and its market experienced growth for several subsequent years. In 1930, electricity use in Edmonton hit new highs: the average home consumed 600 kWh per year, double the amount used in 1910. Edmonton Light and Power had 20,073 customers, up from 19,400 the year before; electric lighting was a common feature in city businesses, public institutions, theatres, and restaurants. That year, plans were underway to introduce "white-way" lighting to Edmonton's business district, to brighten areas once lit by only one lamp per street corner. Ninety-eight additional streetlights were installed in the city's core.

Electricity was being used for less practical purposes. In 1930, Edmonton's Industrial Association recommended that "the city's main streets should be given a festive appearance during the Christmas and New Year's seasons." How? Using coloured lights and brightly lit Christmas trees.

By 1931, Edmonton had a population of over 79,000. Goods that had once been available only in the East could now be purchased in Edmonton. Men could buy ready-made wool suits for $15.75 at the Bond Clothes Shop, while three-piece wool outfits for women were $7.95 at the Hudson's Bay Company store. A 10-pound prime sirloin roast cost $1.30; a pound of butter sold for $0.24.

BELOW: *Many new streetlights were installed along Jasper Avenue in 1930.*

MILESTONES

1930
The RCMP begin policing Alberta as the provincial police are disbanded.

1931
The oldest section of the Rossdale Power Plant is demolished to make way for new equipment.

1932
Rossdale Power Plant sells 51,703,200 kWh to other City of Edmonton departments.

The price of wheat drops to $0.38 a bushel. Prices were $1.60 a bushel in 1929.

1933
Edmonton's first traffic light is installed at Jasper Avenue and 101 Street.

1935
William Aberhart is elected premier of Alberta.

1937
On May 12, a streetcar is decorated with bunting and electric lights as part of Edmonton's celebration of the coronation of King George VI.

Rossdale Power Plant sells 61,028,800 kWh to other City of Edmonton departments.

However, Alberta would not be exempt from the Great Depression for long. By 1932, over 40,000 Albertans worked on government relief projects. By 1933, at least one out of every five workers in Canada had lost their jobs to the economic downturn. Edmonton's power utility was faced with a set of problems it had never experienced before. Demand for power was waning; while it did not decrease, it grew at a much lower rate than had been customary. Despite this, Rossdale struggled, and sometimes failed, to keep up with demand; much of its outdated machinery was working beyond capacity.

A New Boiler

Edmonton's City commissioners continued to plan for a $2 million expansion of Rossdale, as recommended by Superintendent Cunningham in the 1920s. However, this plan would proceed at a

TOP: *The Rossdale Power Plant as it appeared before demolition to make room for boiler number 2.*

MIDDLE LEFT: *This dated stone, which was on the west wall of the power plant, is the only surviving remnant of the 1908 building.*

MIDDLE RIGHT: *Demolition of the old plant began in 1931.*

RIGHT: *Construction of the addition to Rossdale in 1931.*

BELOW: *Number 2 boiler drum was among the new equipment installed in Rossdale.*

RELIEF WORKERS

The Great Depression was a devastating time for the people of Alberta. The price of wheat was at its lowest point in history. Many farmers lost their farms to bank foreclosures. Grasshoppers and drought destroyed millions of acres of crops, sending family farms into ruin. Thousands of men and boys rode the rails in search of jobs.

In 1930, the federal government passed the Relief Act, which allowed unemployed workers to receive small amounts of financial assistance in exchange for work on public projects. "Relief workers" were paid as little as $0.20 a day for doing hard physical labour. In 1932, some of these relief workers helped renovate the Rossdale Power Plant to accommodate the massive boiler and stoker purchased by the City of Edmonton.

The jobless seemed to be everywhere. By 1932, over 40,000 Albertans were on relief. In the fall of that year, a crowd of 13,000 marched to the legislature in Edmonton to protest unemployment. The workers wanted jobs and free medical care; they wanted to present a list of such demands to the premier. Instead, they were beaten back by police. The protest had little immediate effect.

much slower rate than Cunningham had advised.

In 1931, Edmonton City Council approved an expenditure of $450,000 for the purchase of new boiler equipment. This machinery was badly needed; as Cunningham stated in a report to council,

The boiler plant, which in 1914 was considered inadequate, so much so that a new plant was actually designed and contracts awarded, is now producing steam to handle a load more than two and a half times that of 1914.

The new boiler was installed and put into operation by 1932. It was accompanied by a twin stoker (the largest in Canada), and additional coal- and ash-handling equipment. The south end of the power plant was renovated to accommodate the new equipment. However, no new turbines were purchased.

A CATCH-22

The terms of Edmonton's agreement with Calgary Power were negotiated before the effects of the Depression were known. It came into effect on October 1, 1930, and lasted through five of the Depression's worst years. Under the terms of the agreement, Calgary Power sold electricity to Edmonton during the summer, and Edmonton sold surplus power to Calgary Power during the low-water season. Electricity was transmitted along a line installed between Calgary Power's Ghost Plant on the Bow River and Edmonton's Rossdale Power Plant. The deal was advantageous to Calgary Power because its hydro plant produced a surplus during the high-water season. According to Power Plant Superintendent Cunningham, the deal allowed Edmonton to put off the purchase of expensive new equipment and proceed with expansion at a manageable pace. The Great Depression's arrival soon

MILESTONES
(continued)

1938
Clarke Stadium is opened. The 3,000-seat stadium is named after former mayor Joe Clarke.

The owners of Edmonton's Capitol Theatre install the largest theatre marquee in the British Empire. The sign has 2,000 bulbs that can melt snow on the sidewalk below.

On February 11, Local 1007 of the International Brotherhood of Electrical Workers issues its charter. The Edmonton union has 82 members.

Number 1 pumphouse is completed along the river at the Rossdale Power Plant. This building has been preserved to this day.

Jewish people are attacked across Germany on the night of November 9. So many windows are shattered during the violence that the night becomes known as "Kristallnacht."

1939
On September 10, Canada declares war on Germany. Recruitment of soldiers begins across Alberta.

Edmonton begins its first use of trolley buses on September 24.

Number 1 boiler, the largest stoker-fired boiler in Canada, is commissioned at Rossdale.

BELOW: *Life in the city: aboard an Edmonton streetcar in the 1930s.*

BOTTOM: *Vehicles like these were the pride of the Electric Light and Power Department during the 1930s.*

made the Calgary Power agreement seem especially fortuitous.

The deal was not intended to replace Rossdale, but rather to supplement it. Even when electricity was flowing north from the Ghost River plant, Rossdale remained in operation, albeit at a decreased capacity, to operate the water pumping and filtration plants. Rossdale also provided a ready backup in case of an outage on the transmission line. In the first two years of the agreement, Rossdale generated 44,779,800 kWh of electricity, while 56,479,800 kWh were purchased from Calgary Power.

The Calgary deal worked, on paper, to the benefit of both companies; but it assumed that demand for electricity would continue unabated. Unfortunately, demand fell along with the economy. Edmonton was not able to sell its power at the level expected. The pact between the two utilities no longer seemed as profitable as first predicted.

The agreement was due to terminate on October 1, 1935. As this date approached, the merits of the deal were debated in local media. Many participants in this debate felt that the agreement had cost Edmonton both money and jobs. Others knew that the agreement was necessary, regardless of the cost. Though Rossdale had for years made money for the City, relatively little had been reinvested in it. In a report dated February 1934, Power Plant Superintendent Cunningham placed the facts before City Council: the equipment at Rossdale was dangerously obsolete and barely adequate to maintain power to the city. If any piece of aging machinery broke down, the city would face power outages. Basing his estimates on conservative projections of a one-percent annual growth in demand, Cunningham wrote, "It is obvious that an addition to the plant is necessary if it is to function alone – considering even the lowest estimate of growth."

Whose Wire Was It?

March 24, 1930

A.G. Shute, Chief Constable
City Police Department

Re: Police Auto No 2 damaged

Sir,
About 8:50 AM this date I was driving Police Car in answer to a complaint of Mr. De Vall and was going North on 108 A. St. and when I came to CPR tracks I turned East on land between 87th and 88th Ave. (a good traveled road). The Sun was shining very strong on the windshield and I did not see a loose guy wire attached to a Electric Pole and the other end fastened to a hook close by the road.

The top of Auto hit this wire and almost broke it off also broke the windshield. The wire was across the road. I took Auto to No 2 Station and then to Civic Garage.

This wire is very dangerous to the persons who are driving cars on this road. And some person is liable to get hurt.

Later Inspector Robinson and I visited this place and he corroborates my statement. Inspector Robinson recommends that the Electric Dept. be notified to take this wire down and save further accidents.

Yours respectfully,
U. Walker

March 26, 1930

His Worship Mayor J.M. Douglas
Police Commissioner
Edmonton, Alta.

Sir:
I am enclosing herewith copy of report of Constable Walker covering damage done to the South Side Ford car.

The top of the car ... was completely broken off, and all the bows were broken. The uprights which support the windshield were badly bent, and the windshield was broken ... a new top ... will be required, and the uprights supporting the windshield will have to be straightened, the cost of repairing this damage being estimated at $35.00.

The scene of this accident was checked up by the Deputy Chief Constable, and it appears that in the land East of 109th Street and running parallel with the CPR tracks are a number of telegraph poles. On the north side of the land where the accident occurred, one of the poles has a guy wire extending from part way up the pole to the south side of the lane, and there is just barely sufficient room for a car to pass under it. The lane is in poor condition between the guy wire and the post, ruts being very deep there, and it appears quite likely that Constable Walker, in endeavoring to avoid the ruts, struck the wire.

While there may have been a certain element of negligence in this particular case, it would appear that the sun, at the time or the morning when the accident occurred, was shining directly in the driver's eyes, and that the wire could not be seen. This wire is exceedingly dangerous ... at night time it would be quite impossible for the driver of a car to see it. I do not know to whom the telegraph post belongs, but I am forwarding a copy of this report to the City Engineer, as, on account of its dangerous location, this wire should be removed.

Your obedient servant,
A.G. Shute,
Chief Constable,
Edmonton Police Department

March 28, 1930

Mr. D. Mitchell
City Commissioner
City

Re: Accident South Side Police Auto

Dear Sir:
With further reference to our conversation of recent date, re: damage occurring to Auto owned by the City Police in lane East of 109 Street between 87th and 88 Avenues, we beg to advise that upon investigation we find that this Guy wire is owned by the CPR Telegraph Company, and is not used by any of the City Departments.

We would suggest that before writing the CPR Co. on the subject that the Engineer's Department establish whether the present road in on the CPR right-of-way, or whether it is part of one of the City lanes. As this property is more or less in a wild state, it is impossible for the writer to state definitely whether this is CPR right-of-way, or City's lane.

Yours truly,
W. Barnhouse, Superintendent
Electric Light and Power Department

BELOW: *Many Albertans could not afford to operate automobiles in the 1930s. By the middle of the decade, Bennett Buggies, car chassis converted to wagons, were a common sight.*

The City was now in a catch-22 situation. If the agreement with Calgary Power was not renewed, the City would be in an extremely vulnerable position. However, to many City of Edmonton managers, it seemed that the pact was no longer in Edmonton's best interests. The deal was costing the City more than some argued it was worth.

Cunningham proposed that the City continue the development program it had begun two years earlier with the purchase of the new boiler. The predicted cost of the new extension was roughly $1,200,000. A few months after he presented these recommendations, Cunningham died suddenly of a massive stroke. Alex Ritchie, the new acting superintendent, was left to carry the ball for the Rossdale Power Plant.

A NEW PLAYER

Alex Ritchie had an impressive résumé. As an engineer, he had overseen many improvements to the Rossdale Power Plant between 1913 and 1927. He left Rossdale in 1927 to work as a research engineer with a local firm, but returned in 1932 as chief construction engineer during the installation of number 2 boiler. In a January 28, 1927 letter to City Commissioner Mitchell, Superintendent Cunningham described Ritchie as a man who gave "himself loyally and whole-heartedly to the interests of the City." Ritchie is also credited with "securing operating economies, which have resulted in the saving of very considerable money [for] the City."

Unfortunately, Ritchie walked into a hornet's nest when he became acting superintendent. At the time, Edmonton's City commissioners and City Council were still struggling with the Calgary Power Agreement. Adding its voice to the debate was a lobby group known as the Edmonton Tax Research Bureau. The group placed submissions before City Council protesting the interconnection agreement. One of the flyers the group distributed proclaimed:

Taxpayers! Do Not Be Fooled. Based on investigations from every angle possible

BELOW: *This railway crane was used to move coal and ash at Rossdale.*

the old Calgary Power Agreement proved to be — Not an interchange agreement but a "short change" agreement. So why renew it?

The Edmonton Tax Research Bureau argued that Edmonton paid for its power twice under the Calgary Power agreement: one payment went to Calgary Power and the other to Edmonton Power's workers, who maintained Rossdale year-round. Ritchie disagreed with the Bureau's assessment. He argued that the agreement had saved Edmonton $192,793 in the two-year period ending in 1932.

"FIGHTING JOE" ENTERS THE DEBATE

A new mayor was elected during this debate. "Fighting Joe Clarke," as he was popularly called, promptly criticized the work of Acting Superintendent Ritchie.

Like his predecessor, Ritchie estimated that a 20,000-kW extension to the Rossdale Power Plant would cost over $1 million. City Council approved this expenditure in June 1935. However, Mayor Clarke publicly called Ritchie's estimate into question (along with his credentials), suggesting that $600,000 would be more than enough to cover the cost of the plant expansion.

Clarke's scapegoating tactics did nothing to resolve the situation. Council decided against renewing the Calgary Power agreement, which allowed the City only one year to do a three-year job – updating Rossdale. Yet, no concrete action was taken to commence the update.

This situation caused great concern in Edmonton's business community. Canadian National Railways, one of the utility's largest customers, argued that

LEFT: *This substation, located at 104 Street and 83 Avenue, was destroyed by an explosion in 1936.*

any interruption of power would mean closing plants and laying off workers. Newspapers fuelled fears with headlines like "Sees Danger in Condition of Edmonton Power Plant."

In March 1936, an explosion demolished a new automatic substation located at 104 Street and 83 Avenue, and fanned fears about the state of Edmonton's electrical utility. The explosion was caused by a leaky transformer, and was unrelated to the functioning of the power plant. While the Rossdale Power Plant provided an emergency circuit to affected areas, power was not completely restored for a few days.

TOO LITTLE, TOO LATE

On April 13, 1936, only a few days after the connection with Calgary Power Ltd. was severed, the city called for tenders on a 15,000-kW turbo-generator for the Rossdale Power Plant. Newspaper reports noted that "commissioners have not yet determined how the costly extension will be financed."

Then the inevitable occurred. On May 26, 1936, a blowout in a thick feeder cable leading from the main 10,000-kW turbine to the control room of the power plant resulted in the unit being out of commission for nearly two hours. Across the city, streetcars stopped, water service was cut off, and packing plants, dairies, flourmills, and grain companies stopped work. Power was eventually restored, but only for 24 hours – this was only the first of three breakdowns. On May 27, a second feeder cable broke and power was cut off for 25 minutes. Then, on May 28, trouble at the Rossdale Power Plant led to the third breakdown in three days.

Now Edmonton's civic leaders were in the spotlight. Groups like the Canadian Manufacturers' Association were asking the mayor to explain the power breakdowns. They also wanted to know what measures he was taking to ensure that the breakdowns weren't repeated. City Council looked for someone to blame, and Alex Ritchie was singled out as the author of the utility's troubles.

In August 1936, in a six-to-five vote (with the mayor casting the deciding ballot), City Council ousted Alex Ritchie from his job as acting power plant superintendent. Edmonton newspaper editorials condemned what was clearly a political decision designed to deflect responsibility for the outages away from City Council.

Alex Ritchie may have found some consolation in the elections held a year later, which ousted Joe Clarke, his nemesis, from office. Around the same time, City Council backtracked and established a new agreement with Calgary Power Ltd. Now both utilities would provide each other with "standby" power for emergency use. The agreement was effective for one year, and could be terminated with a month's notice.

A new superintendent, Robert G. Watson, was hired to replace Ritchie. Terry Stone, a former employee, remembers Watson as a tough-minded "dapper man with an Adolf Menjou moustache."

WHAT TO DO WHEN THE LIGHTS GO OUT

Madame M. Dey of Madame Dey's Beauty Parlour spoke about the impact of the power outage on May 27, 1936:

"I have been in business 12 years and never before have I been without power for such a long time. It is certainly fortunate that no one was being treated by our permanent wave machines when the power went off."

From The Edmonton Journal, *1936*

The Rossdale Power Plant

The Rossdale Power Plant is a good example of the architectural design, style, and construction methods that were used in the late 1920s and 1930s. The building was constructed using some of the new products of the time, including metal decking, open web steel joists, steel-framed windows, and pre-cast concrete. The reinforced concrete foundations, structural steel framing system, and non-load-bearing masonry walls met the unique design requirements for modern electrical power plants of the time.

The building is a good example of the use of shop-built steelwork and reflects the high level of consistency and precision associated with this construction method. This type of construction lent itself to expansion over the history of the building with virtually no modification to the construction system or details.

Architect David Whiting describes the Rossdale Power Plant as having an excellent example of notable or rare architectural style. The plant reflects traditional elements of classical architectural design. Base, column, and pediment are interpreted in the Rossdale design in a manner unique to the early 1900s.

Adapted from Historic Resource Impact Assessment, Rossdale Power Plant, *by David Whiting, 1999*

BELOW: *The Rossdale Power Plant as it appeared near the end of the 1930s. The structure that is visible in this photograph, with the exception of the coal-handling equipment attached to the building's exterior, remained standing in 2002. Note the railway tracks in the photograph foreground; rail cars were used to haul coal within reach of the loading crane, visible on the far left of the photograph.*

Working Conditions

In the 1930s, industrial working conditions were much poorer than they are today. Terry Stone began to work at the Rossdale Power Plant in 1938 as an apprentice electrician. "It was a dungeon," says Stone. "We had to work in coal dust and dirt from bunkers above and the smell of coal gas. The ash pit was like something from the industrial revolution." Asbestos was still used as insulation on pipes, and Stone recalls flakes of the substance floating in the air inside the plant. One of his jobs was to clean and sweep out the switch room on

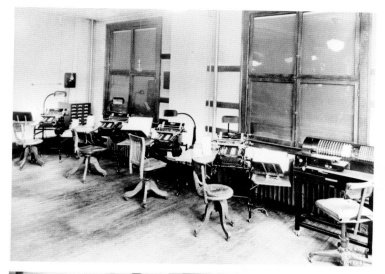

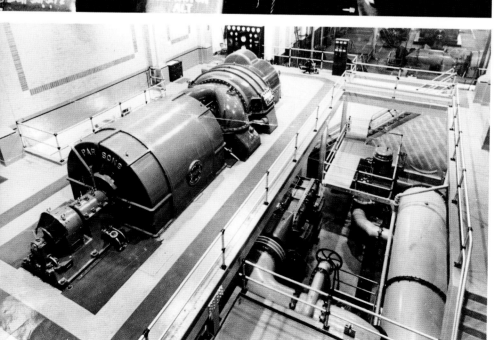

ABOVE: *Utility bills flowed from this office (left) and were payable at the Civic Block (right).*

LEFT: *Parsons generator number 1 was installed at Rossdale in 1939. Chief Engineer Bill Darby watched as the low-pressure boiler casing was lowered into place.*

BOTTOM: *The 15,000-kW generator as it appeared after installation.*

Saturdays. "In the old switch rooms it was all open bus-bars," says Stone, shaking his head. "It wasn't until 1947 or 1948 that we got metal-clad switch gear."

Despite technological advances, much of the work at the power plant in the 1930s still involved old-fashioned physical labour. "They used heavy lead-covered cables at that time," says Stone. "It took a strong man to lift a six-foot length. We had to get a truck to pull the cables in." Stone's starting wage was $0.33 cents an hour for a 44-hour week. "Just having a job during the Depression was good," he says.

RECOVERY

By 1937, demand for power was again rising. Superintendent Watson reported an increase of 695,200 kWh for the first four months of the year, compared to the

In the 1930s, the Billing Section of the City of Edmonton was located in the Civic Block on 99 Street and 102 Avenue. The section employed eight meter readers and a bill delivery person. Another staff person took applications over the counter and was responsible for collecting a $3 deposit for light and a $3 deposit for water. Customers who brought the title of their property to the office weren't charged the water deposit. Businesses were charged a $5 deposit for light.

Domestic customers could apply for a "combination rate." To qualify, the customer was required to have five electric appliances. It wasn't uncommon for many customers to borrow a toaster and iron from a neighbour to qualify!

Each customer account included a meter sheet. Staff used these to record meter numbers for both power and water, the class for calculating charges, the readings, consumption, and charges for the last twelve months. The sheets also included remarks from the meter reader about the location of meters, whether or not the customer owned a dog, and if the occupant was friendly or otherwise.

In a May 1935 letter, Superintendent Barnhouse of the Electric Light and Power Department responds to a request for a special meter reading:

From time to time requests are made by consumers asking that their meters be read on certain dates to suit their convenience. We are unable to accede to these requests owing to the extra cost,

and the resulting disarrangement to a predetermined schedule.

All meters are read on a definite schedule divided into 125 districts. Total meters read in January: Electric Light Department 21,466; Water 14,151 – an average of 1,148 meters per day at an average cost of 2.72 cents per meter. Of the total number of meters, only 149 are read out of the regular schedule. These special readings cost an average of 12.6 cents per meter, and cover the large industrial accounts, railways, government, and are read at the end of each month.

Requests for special readings make it very difficult for billing etc. For example, a reading taken several days before or after the regular schedule means the adding to, or deducting from the total amount charged to the district in question. Any additional expense is that of mailing all special readings and the extension of time allowed for discount, i.e., 99 consumers in a certain district, the discount may expire on the 10th day of the month, and one special on the 16th day of the month.

It will be seen from the foregoing explanation that such requests all tend to throw the schedule of reading, billing etc. out of step, and thereby increase the cost.

Sources: Billing Department Files, Letter from W. Barnhouse to D. Mitchell

same period in the previous year. With the Depression on the wane, the City finally took real steps to redevelop the power plant. By March 1939, a new $215,000 Parsons 15,000-kW turbo-generator (number 1) had been installed in a renovated and expanded Rossdale Power Plant. A $220,000 boiler (number 1) capable of generating 155,000 pounds of steam an hour – the largest in Canada at the time – was also purchased.

As the 1930s drew to a close, Edmonton's power plant seemed to once again be in excellent condition to meet the power needs of a growing city. In the coming decade, the utility would face a new challenge: not economic decline, but wartime demand.

"600" DESIGNATION SAID 'JUST SWANK'

What is the meaning of the "600" appearing on the front of the new electric light substation at 124 Street and 107 Ave?

It doesn't mean there are 600 such substations in Edmonton, Electric Light Supt. William Barnhouse said Friday, answering a question that has been puzzling inquisitive west-enders.

"It's just a designating number we use in the department, but there's no particular reason why we call it 600 rather than just six," Mr. Barnhouse said. There are only seven such substations in the city, he added.

From The Edmonton Journal, *1938*

CHAPTER 5

Holding the Line

. . . . .

1940 – 1949

$\mathcal{D}$emand for power surged in Edmonton during the 1940s, and Rossdale was obliged to keep up. Edmonton, with its busy aviation fields, was a key part of Canada's war effort, and much of Alberta's industry was adapted to wartime production. Coal and labour shortages, both resulting from the war, hampered electricity production. Edmonton itself also grew in size. Through all of these challenges, however, Edmonton's power plant proved itself to be a dependable and innovative source of electricity.

A NEW DEAL

Once again, an offer to exchange surplus energy with Calgary Power was on the table in 1939. And, as in previous decades, debate over this offer was heated. The issue was urgent during the war years; it was vital that electricity continue to flow uninterrupted to the city and its wartime industries.

Many thought that Edmonton had found its own solution to the electric supply problem when it increased total

BELOW: *Jasper Avenue in 1942.*

1940
Edmonton's Commercial Grads basketball club plays its last game.

The Canadian Standards Association assumes responsibility for testing electrical equipment for safety.

1942
The Alaska Highway is constructed.

A record-breaking snowfall ties up city traffic.

1943
Eight hundred and sixty planes pass through Edmonton on September 23, setting a North American record.

1945
World War II ends. The Loyal Edmonton Regiment returns home.

1947
Oil is discovered near Leduc.

Edmonton's electrical utility commissions the Network Distribution System in downtown Edmonton.

1948
The Edmonton Flyers hockey club wins the Allan Cup, the Canadian senior amateur title.

The Northern Canada Power Commission is created.

installed capacity to 38,000 kW. It accomplished this with the installation of turbo-generator number 1. City Council had also approved the installation of a $750,000 generator in 1941. With such a capacity for production, many felt that a pact with Calgary Power was not only unnecessary but also undesirable, given the negative press that the collaboration had been given in the 1930s.

Proponents of the agreement were concerned about coal shortages, war demands, increased population growth, and the very real threat of power outages. Arguing that an interchange agreement with Calgary Power would assist Edmonton in times of shortage or outage, those in favour of an agreement pressed for a decision.

That argument was given additional weight on Saturday, August 10, 1940, at 1:00 PM, when a major power breakdown struck Edmonton. All over the city, streetcars stalled and water was shut off. The cause: a blown cable and motor that drove a fan on a main steam boiler at Rossdale. Deputy Mayor Guy Paterson accepted an offer from Calgary Power to provide electricity to Edmonton free of charge for the duration of the crisis; in doing so, he overruled R.G. Watson, Rossdale superintendent. In the end, Rossdale was brought back into operation before Calgary sent any power northward.

This outage prompted City Council to act. After a series of late-night meetings and discussions, the council finally voted six-four in favour of the Calgary Power agreement on August 28, 1940.

EXPANSION AT ROSSDALE

Despite a renewed agreement with Calgary Power, expansion at the Rossdale Power Plant remained an issue. In March 1940, City Council approved an additional $750,000 improvement to the power plant in the form of renovations and new equipment. Calls for tenders were released and Superintendent Watson made inquiries about the pur-

chase of a 15,000-kW turbine (number 2) from C.A. Parsons and Company Limited in England.

By the fall of 1940, however, City Council had decided to delay action on the proposed power extension program for three months. There seemed to be serious objection to the issue; the Edmonton Taxpayers Association argued against expansion, citing the need to support the British war effort through reducing municipal taxes so that citizens could bear a growing federal war tax. Others countered that a turbine purchase from Britain would increase British exports and help to maintain British foreign trade.

In October 1940, just one month into the three-month delay, another surprising turn of events obliged City Council to revisit its decision to delay. City commissioners announced that a

representative of the Canadian and British governments had asked Edmonton to proceed immediately with a $730,000 extension to the City-owned power plant so as to help supply power for the $8,000,000 ammonium nitrate plant planned in southern Alberta as part

THE INTERCHANGE AGREEMENT CLAUSE

Subject to the requirements of the City to supply itself and its present and future customers, and to the present capacity of its steam plant, the City shall supply any kilowatt hours to the company [Calgary Power] which the company may require during the low water seasons; and subject only to the company's ability to supply from its present hydro-electric plants, the company agrees to accept such kilowatt hours as and when required by the City during subsequent high-water seasons; and during such high-water seasons the City for such periods as may be necessary to permit the company to return the kilowatt hours due to the City and/or to permit the company to establish a kilowatt hour credit balance as provided for, agrees to operate its steam plant at loads not exceeding 4,000 kW, or at such greater loads as may be necessary from time to time to supply itself and present and future customers and which the company is unable to supply or may be mutually agreed upon to meet the circumstances then existing ....

from The Edmonton Journal

of the Canadian government's wartime explosives program.

Ammonium nitrate is used in making smokeless and flameless explosives.

Though the ammonium nitrate plant was also negotiating with Calgary Power, it was clear that an expansion of Rossdale was necessary; war industries all over the province would need more electrical power. The decision to move forward with the expansion was made. Superintendent Watson arranged for the purchase of a new boiler and turbine. The boiler, made in Galt, Ontario by Babcock & Wilcox, arrived in the fall of 1941 at a cost of $244,000. The British turbine cost $258,000. The balance of the expansion budget was spent on equipment needed to make the new turbine and boiler operational, and on an expansion of the building at Rossdale.

Portions of the British turbine were delivered in August, 1942; however, the rest went down in the Atlantic along with the transport ship, both victims of

BELOW: *A view of the interior of the Rossdale Power Plant. Parsons turbine-generators numbers 1 and 2 are the two similar machines on the upper level. Generators commissioned before World War I are visible in the background.*

ALBERTA'S CHEMICAL INDUSTRY

The basic chemical industry was founded in the province in 1941, when a plant was built at Calgary to produce ammonia and ammonium nitrate, using natural gas as the principal raw material. Before the end of the Second World War this plant was converted to the manufacture of ammonia and fertilizer-grade ammonium nitrate. In 1952, an industrial high explosives plant commenced operation at Calgary, using ammonia and ammonium nitrate from the fertilizer plant.

From Alberta: Province of Opportunity

ABOVE: *Edmonton's streets were well lit in the 1940s.*

RIGHT: *Edmonton power plant employee Frank Prior inspecting a switchboard at Rossdale in 1944.*

Nazi submarines, in December 1942. C.A. Parsons replaced the parts, which arrived at last in May of 1943. R.G. Watson was able to put the full system into operation by March, 1944.

The expansion was timely. Rossdale's output in September of 1942 was 36.3 percent greater than output in the same period in 1941. Much of this electricity was sent south to Calgary Power under the terms of the interchange agreement. Edmonton's own war efforts were increasing consumption locally as well. Airport construction, aircraft repair,

Transcript of a CJCA Broadcast

March 3, 1943 at 9:30 PM
Announcer: Tonight's "Town Topics" originate at the city power plant, the heart of Edmonton's intricate system of electricity and water supply. We are standing now at the site of the City's efficient and up-to-date plant that supplies your homes, offices and industrial centres with lighting, electrical power, and water. This plant originally operated from the river's edge at the foot of 101st street. It was moved in 1907 to its present location. At that time it was already the property of the City of Edmonton for three years. Since 1907, the plant grew as the city grew, increasing its capacity for generating electricity from 4,000 kWh to 34,000 kWh. This maximum capacity will be increased as soon as another 15,000 kWh generator can be installed. First impression we get as we enter this huge building is the immensity of the machinery coupled with the physical insignificance of man in their midst. The deafening drone of the turbines helps make the man's position in the midst of this huge machinery even more insignificant. We'll start in the boiler room, where the resulting power in your home or factory passes through its first stages of creation.

Pause to reach boiler room.
Towering above us for 60 feet are three boilers, two of them now being in operation, and the third, nearing completion. These are tremendous objects with goose-walks and stairways draping the sides and ends. Running full-length along the lower front side are the stokers which are fed by a coal hopper or "way line" which is suspended from a rail and stretches out its crane-full of coal towards the stokers as it supplies the required amount of coal. The coal is automatically weighed as it passes out of an overhead bunker into the travelling way line. It passes through a crusher before it reaches the overhead bunker. Situated right behind us at a point from which all three boilers can readily be seen is the control panel, which automatically charts water level, air flow, coal consumption, steam pressure, and so on. This of course is the guide for the automatic control of the huge stokers. Now, coming out of this immense and complicated set-up and bringing the results to your home, here's what the results are: every pound of coal and every 9 1/4 pounds of water used in this room supply you with enough electricity to burn 10-100 W bulbs for one hour. Now to see how that tremendous amount of electricity is made [we go] into the next room.

Pause.
Here we see the source of that droning noise you likely hear, and the source of your electricity. We're standing alongside the newest acquisition to your city's plant. The immense 15,000 kWh generator was installed several years ago. It's a huge cylinder laying horizontally with a portion of the lower regions below the floor surface. At the far end of this long room is the 10,000 kW turbine and alongside are the 4- and 5,000 ones. The two small turbines are idle now, as with the lengthening day, the city demand for power has receded from the mid-winter peak. Standing in this same line of monster machines is the Direct Current Reciprocating Steam Engine, which augments power for the city street railway. All these are immense machines. Standing at this elevated point, they give one a scene that could well be compared with a number of dinosaurs or whales wallowing in shallow water. We'll step over to our right a short distance to see what's below us.

Pause.
Looking over a strong rail we see huge pipes, one about six feet in diameter and one about four – serving as a lead-in and an outlet for the water supply at the plant. The smaller pipe leads to the condenser. That's a bulky machine whose job it is to change the steam coming out of the turbines back into water. It's the pivot link in the chain which forms the water cycle at the plant. Here's how the water travels. It's heated in the boilers and is passed to the turbines, at very near the boiling point. In the process of generating electricity it changes into steam and is passed to the condenser in that form. The condenser changes it back to water, whence it returns to the boilers to complete the cycle. Simple, isn't it?

Pause.
Lining a high wall above us is a long series of panels bedecked with dials, switches, buttons and numerous other gadgets. These are the switchboards which control the lighting and power supply in various parts of the city. Here's Mr. R.G. Watson, plant superintendent ... Thanks very kindly, Mr. Watson, and the best of success with your regular operations and your new installations.

Back to studio for signoff.

Note that many of the figures and some of the processes given in the transcript are incorrect. The generating station was relocated to the Rossdale site in 1902. The generating capacity figures were 1907, 1908, and 1943 were, respectively, 675 kW, 1,375 kW, and 38,000 kW.

TWO WOMEN METER READERS LIKE THEIR WARTIME WORK

Edmonton's two women meter readers, Mrs. Verna Barnett and Mrs. Ruth Limb, like their jobs despite fierce-looking dogs, strange basements and dusty meters.

They've been on the job for three weeks, and they don't look at the winter months ahead with misgiving.

"I guess some days won't be so nice what with cold winds and deep snow ... but then, it's all part of the job," says Mrs. Barnett. Mrs. Barnett wears blue coveralls on her job now but the City is making plans to equip all the meter readers, including the two women, with fleece-lined parkas for the winter months.

"I find the people very nice to deal with as I go from house to house," Mrs. Barnett declared. "I haven't had any trouble with dogs yet and don't expect any. I find that no matter how tough they look, if you speak to them in a friendly fashion they don't bother you."

"I suppose you see some pretty fantastic basements as you go around?" asked the reporter.

"Well, I wouldn't like to say," she replied. "What people have in their basements and how they keep them is their own business, I guess."

A goodly number of the meters are dusty and Mrs. Barnett said sometimes she has to get a rag and wipe the glass clear so she can read them.

"The funny part of it is," she added, "after getting this job I checked up on the condition of my own meter and have to admit I found it pretty dirty. You don't realize these things until you become personally interested."

The City employs eight meter readers under foreman S. Clark. Mr. Clark thinks his two women readers are "just fine."

from The Edmonton Journal, *1943*

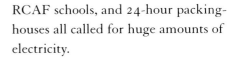

RCAF schools, and 24-hour packing-houses all called for huge amounts of electricity.

TWO WOMEN HIRED AS METER READERS

Another challenge that the utility faced during the war years was a critical shortage of workers. In August 1943, plans were announced to hire two women as meter readers. In an August 31 *Edmonton Journal* report, it was made clear that this move was intended to supplement male meter readers, not replace them. Much attention was paid to the problem of outfitting the female workers; the City hoped to provide the women with coveralls and a cap.

COAL SHORTAGES

During the early 1940s, the cost and availability of coal provided another challenge to the City's ability to produce adequate power. North America's war machine consumed vast amounts of coal. It is therefore no surprise that the price of coal had almost doubled by the end of the war, going from $1.58/ton in 1939 to $3.11/ton in 1945. The implications of this shortage for Rossdale were serious. In December of 1942 the power plant's coal reserve was reduced to 7,000 tons, down from 14,000 tons. The possibility of power rationing became very real because the plant used 300 tonnes of coal per day in peak season.

In November 1943, a miner's strike reduced coal reserves to such low levels that the City had to declare a "dimout" to conserve the fuel. Streetlights were off longer, and citizens, businesses, and

LEFT: *Pre-World War I machines continued to operate in the Rossdale Power Plant through the 1940s.*

ABOVE: *Roy Fitzsimmons (left) and Stan Hampton (right) at 350 Substation.*

industries were asked to reduce the amount of electricity they used as much as possible. Watson was able to obtain between 5,000 and 10,000 tons of coal from an abandoned mine near Camrose, which was expected to see the plant through a few weeks. By December 1, 1943, Watson had built the reserve up sufficiently to ease up on the city-wide dimout.

The coal shortage gave rise to the first of many discussions about converting some or all of Rossdale's boilers into gas-fired burners. In letters to and from City commissioners, the mayor, aldermen, coal company representatives, and R.G. Watson argued back and forth through-out July and August of 1943, sometimes quite heatedly. The need to protect the multi-million dollar coal industry, the inability of the gas company to provide enough gas, and Watson's uncertainty about possible damage to the boilers all

worked together to argue against using gas. On August 20, 1943, R.J. Gibb, commissioner of utilities, wrote to Ernest Manning, minister of trade and industry, in response to Manning's inquiry about conversion to gas: "[T]he Civic Administration was never very favorable to the proposed change. The matter seems to be in abeyance and if it is revised we will be pleased to advise you." For now, the question was at rest.

By March of 1944, coal reserves had increased to 18,000 tons and power plant officials were no longer concerned about shortages.

EXPANSION

Rossdale's expansion in 1944 didn't quench Alberta's thirst for electricity. By May 1945, Watson was before City Council with another request for expansion to the power plant. The need was much greater this time. In the five years since his previous request, Edmonton's population had increased from 91,723 to

BOMB SCARE WRECKS METER FOR CITY LIGHT DEPARTMENT

Because an Edmonton hotel owner was bomb-shy early Thursday, the City Electric Light Department is shy one voltage checking meter.

Shortly after 4:00 AM a guest at the Banff Hotel, 9930 Jasper Avenue, awoke proprietor Morris Gottfriend excitedly, telling him he had found "a bomb" ticking away in the hall. It precipitated a bomb scare, as Gottfriend on checking found a 12-inch by 16-inch box plugged into the electrical system in the hotel hallway.

When he heard the box ticking ominously, Gottfriend took no chances. Instead he took the box in his hands, ripped it away from the wall and tossed it out of a window onto an adjoining roof.

Then he ran as fast as he could to the police station two blocks away and burst in to report the "bomb." Constables Benny Wheatfield and W. A. Maloney rushed to the hotel as a two-man demolition squad, and finally found the "bomb" on the next door roof.

It was ticking no longer. In fact, chances were it would never tick again, which is why the Electric Light Department is out some equipment. The "bomb" turned out to be a clock-work meter the department uses to check electrical systems in Edmonton buildings. Tossing it out of a window onto a roof did it little good.

from The Edmonton Journal, *1949*

111,745. Power demand was continually on the rise. Watson also argued that a cheap and reliable power source would attract more industry to Edmonton. He outlined a $1,777,000 expansion that included a new 30,000-kW turbine generator and associated boiler and auxiliaries, all of which could be paid for by the end of 1949 with reserves from revenues.

In September 1945, City Council approved Watson's expansion program,

BELOW: *Transformers for the new Network Distribution System arrived by train.*

BOTTOM: *Ducts such as these were essential in the Network Distribution System.*

BELOW RIGHT: *Transformers were lowered into vaults below city sidewalks.*

and by 1949 generator number 3 and boiler number 5 were installed and operational. According to employee Terry Stone, the installation of this equipment had some interesting challenges:

On a Saturday in 1948 there was a cloud burst over the river valley, and you couldn't see 20 feet in front of you. We were bringing in some equipment through an opening in the wall. The rain was leaking in through the roof drains and we had all of these open cables and circuits. We had to use tarps to scoop the water out.

Despite the dangers, no one was hurt and the equipment was safely situated in

the plant. Once things were up and running, says Stone, "there was the constant hum of machines all day long. If there was a little surge in the machines you would pick it up right away." Like so many others who have worked at the plant, Stone's ears were totally tuned in to the noise of the turbines.

POWER DISTRIBUTION TAKES A NEW TURN

In 1947 the Electric Light and Power Department determined that it was time to remove the lines that had long been strung over streets and sidewalks in the downtown core of Edmonton. The lines would be installed in an underground complex called the Network Distribution System. This system was designed

The system diagram, or dummy bus board, in the picture at right is an illustration of the city's electrical distribution system as it was between 1947 and 1957. During this period, the board was mounted in a control room at Rossdale. Each chrome or copper bar on the board represented a feeder coming out of Rossdale; these feeders led to substations around the city, as well as large industrial customers. There were 85 switches on the board; these switches indicated which lines were active.

Circuits could not be controlled from the bus board. In order to activate (or deactivate) a line, the operator would select the appropriate key from a cabinet at Rossdale, drive out into the field, use the key to close or open the circuit, then return to the powerhouse. The switches on the board were then manually moved to the "on" or "off" position.

Adapted from text by Paul Collis

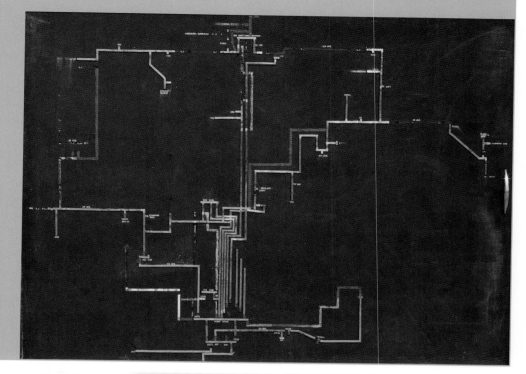

to ensure that electricity could be supplied at the usual voltage even if one or more of the transformers or supply cables shut down or failed. Theoretically, just five of the eight primary cables could supply the network load, if necessary.

A system of vaults and duct lines was built beneath the streets in Edmonton's downtown core. This system housed transformers and cables, and was connected to the surface by manholes. Removable grates and concrete lids from this system remain visible today.

This was a reliable method of power distribution. The underground system

put into place in 1947 would be expanded and improved as the city grew over the next few decades. Subsequent power outages were much less serious than they would have been with an aerial system. According to Art Baird, an engineer and retired director of distribution engineer-

ABOVE: *Rossdale in the 1940s.*

ing, only three major outages (July 1965, August 1973, and March 1979) resulted from failures within the Network Distribution System. Other outages to the network service area occurred when

'I'm Just Sick'

April 2, 1949

Dear City Commissioners:
This is not a joke – I'm just sick.

Enclosed package is only a sample of what I have on my door steps and window sills every day from the city power plant.

Can not anything be done to prevent some of this menace I sure would be very grateful. I have been a resident of this city, since 1901, and love Edmonton and its people;

Sincerely yours
(Mrs.) Christopher Spillios

April 6, 1949

Mrs. Christopher Spillios,
9742 - 103 St.
Edmonton.

Dear Madam,
Received your letter and package as of April 2, and I am quite in agreement with you that the situation is not good.

It is only during the present winter that complaints have been made concerning the power plant and the commissioners and the superintendent, as well as council, have been considering methods which would alleviate the situation. The boiler giving the most difficulty is one which has to be dismantled and cleaned. During the past winter pending the use of new equipment, some of our boilers have been forced in order to produce the necessary power and we think that this may have something to do with the condition.

Commissioner Menzies, who is an engineer, is following up the matter with the superintendent with a view to finding some remedy and I trust that they will be successful.

We are aware of one method but it is pretty costly and in view of the discussion with council concerning the installation of gas in our power plant, there has been some delay in deciding on a definite policy.

Yours very truly,

MAYOR

all generating units shut down as a result of system faults.

Pollution the Issue as Decade Closes

At the close of the decade, air pollution in the form of fly ash would become a major issue for the power plant. Letters began to arrive in Commissioner Menzie's office from Rossdale citizens concerned about fly ash, which drifted down the river valley and onto skating rinks, fresh laundry, and furniture. Residents wanted a solution to the problem.

Superintendent William McFarland, who succeeded Watson in 1945, submitted a report on the issue to City Council. According to McFarland, the problem resulted from forcing old boilers to burn more coal than usual, and was therefore temporary. More coal was burned in the winter of 1948 than ever before, and new boilers were yet to be operational. Therefore, the old boilers operated at lower efficiency and discharged more than the usual amounts of fly ash. It was hoped that installing new boilers would solve the fly ash problem.

In fact, the new boilers aggravated the situation. Because of the new design, less ash was trapped in the boiler and more

Protest Against the Power Plant

Residents of Rossdale Community League are more than just irked, they're fighting mad, and Edmonton's City commissioners are pondering ways to make them mellow again. Blackened housewives' washes, nearly $2,000 worth of unusable rinks, and doctor's bills for removal of cinders from eyes have the Rossdale residents up in arms. Their anger is caused by the belching grit which settles over the district daily from the four smoke stacks of the City's power plant.

Protests against the black dust have been lodged with the commissioners for the past two years. The ire of the residents reached the boiling point this winter when the black cloud became denser. Full blast was given City commissioners Thursday.

Charles Simmonds, president of the Federation of Community Leagues, and Duncan Innes, chairman of the federation's civic committee, took the communities' protests before Commissioner Menzies and demanded that something be done.

from The Edmonton Journal, *1948*

went up the stack! Alterations were made with some positive results, but the problem prevailed.

Technology that would allow the utility to burn coal without producing fly ash was unavailable in the 1940s. Thus, when large quantities of gas were discovered near Leduc in 1947, the City converted some of its boilers to use this cleaner fuel. Number 1 boiler was the first to be converted, and in late November 1949 began to burn gas. By the end of December, City Council was discussing a full conversion to gas. The City would save money on ash-control equipment as well as on fuel costs. However, the topic remained an open issue as the decade closed.

LABOUR SHORTAGES

A labour shortage marked 1949 for the Electric Light and Power Department. Though the war had been over for years, there was a severe shortage of linemen; workers were required to install sorely needed streetlights. According to an *Edmonton Journal*

report, an appeal made to the cities of Vancouver and Winnipeg failed to produce reinforcements for Edmonton's linemen. The department consequently had to turn to all of the employment offices in Canada to request help in remedying the situation. As a result of the labour shortage, streetlighting improvements planned for 99 Street and 109 Street were placed on hold until more men could be found.

Rossdale's capacity was 38,000 kW at the beginning of the 1940s; this was increased to 60,000 kW over the course of the decade. Edmonton's utility was fast becoming a leader in power production technology. In 1949, Rossdale was described as being the largest plant of its kind in Canada; it was well prepared for postwar industrial expansion. To its credit, the utility also responded to concerns about its impact on the environment, and took steps towards reducing air pollution.

BELOW: *Oil was discovered near Leduc in 1947.*

UNDERGROUND TREASURES CHANGE ALBERTA FOREVER

Beginning February 1947, Alberta's economy was no longer dependent on agriculture. The discovery of oil near Leduc forever changed the province.

The number of producing oil wells in Alberta increased from 418 to 7,390 in the decade following the Leduc oilfield discovery, and the petroleum industry pumped $2.5 billion into the Alberta economy. New manufacturing plants went up. Within a few years, pipelines carried oil west to the Pacific and east to the Great Lakes. Thousands of jobs were created, and the population of Edmonton grew rapidly. Edmonton had become the sixth-largest Canadian city by 1956, and along with Calgary, was the fastest growing metropolitan area in Canada.

CHAPTER 6

The Rock 'n' Roll Generation

. . . . .

1950 – 1959

OPPOSITE: *The Rossdale site in the early 1950s.*

Optimism, growth, and faith in technology characterized the 1950s, a decade that greatly contrasted with the bleak war years of the 1940s. People looked to progress as the answer to social ills, and to technology as a means of resolving material challenges. In Edmonton, at least, they were not disappointed: the city basked in oil-fed wealth.

Great strides were made in the production of electricity during the 1950s. Edmonton's power departments became leaders in the industry by installing the very latest in turbines, boilers, underground distribution systems, oil-filled cables, aerial towers, and wires that carried previously unheard of amounts of electricity to businesses and residences.

ROSSDALE EXPANSION

The Edmonton Journal reported that Edmonton's power plant remained "one of the greatest steam generating plants in Canada" in 1950, producing record amounts of electricity. This record pointed to the need for expansion. In fact, expansion would be required throughout the decade: the population of Edmonton was growing fast, nearly doubling from 1950 (148,861) to 1959 (260,733).

In 1950, the string of upgrades began when a new Parsons 30,000-kW turbogenerator and a gas- and oil-fired boiler were ordered. The City of Edmonton approved a $2 million addition to the Rossdale building to make room for the new equipment. Construction was underway in 1951. The older part of the power plant, located on the north end of the complex and dating from the early teens, was demolished. A new section was built in its place. The construction work was completed in 1953, and by September the

MILESTONES

1950
The interprovincial oil pipeline to Ontario is completed.

The Edmonton Mercurys win the World Hockey Championship.

Jasper Place is incorporated as a village.

1951
The Edmonton Bulletin discontinues publication.

1954
CFRN-TV, Edmonton's first television station, starts operation. Edmonton's electric utility works to provide power to new television sets.

The Edmonton Eskimos win their first Grey Cup.

Many Edmontonians replace their kitchen electrical outlets as new, polarized (three-pronged) receptacles become mandatory.

1955
Construction of Edmonton's Jubilee Auditorium begins.

Groat Bridge is opened.

The Province of Alberta turns 50.

1957
Edmonton's new city hall opens.

ABOVE: *Inside the Low Pressure Plant in 1952.*

new turbo-generator (number 4) and boiler number 6 were installed.

This expansion was more complicated than preceding ones: the addition was built in the middle of the existing plant, and operations at both ends had to continue during construction. The replacement of all existing switchgear and control panels further complicated operation. Despite these challenges, the expansion was much needed and much praised. Superintendent Kirkland opened the new addition to the plant along with Mayor Bill Hawrelak and Premier Ernest Manning. Before lighting the fire that set the new boiler into

action, Premier Manning described the event as "another milestone in the progress of a great city."

Though ambitious and expensive, this expansion proved to be insufficient even before it was complete. A third 30,000-kW turbine-generator (number 5) was installed in 1955. This was the final installation in what came to be known as the Low Pressure Plant.

Edmonton's growing population also placed an increasing demand on the City's ability to provide water to its citizens. The pumphouse, long a part of the power plant site, now also required expansion. Construction of a new pumping station on the west side of the plant at the river's edge was undertaken

in the mid-1950s, with three 60-inch intake pipes running almost a third of the way into the river. Towards the east end of the site a new water filtration building was also constructed. According to Superintendent Kirkland, all of these changes and additions increased the efficiency of the operation, more than doubling existing water production with no increase in staff.

THE 100-MW MILESTONE
In the mid-1950s, Rossdale's generating capacity exceeded 100 MW. The first day this capacity was utilized remains a milestone in the careers of many employees. George Faulder, a mechanical engineer at the power plant from

ABOVE: *The fleet of vehicles used by City electrical workers in the 1950s.*

1954 to 1966, remembers that day well. "I remember that first time we reached 100 MW around 1955 or 1956," he says. "Everything was just humming."

Electrical engineer Frank Battistella was also part of this event. "That day in late December of '55," he recalls,

we were conducting a full test on turbine-generator number 5 and its boiler, number 7, to determine if the equipment met the contract designs for output and efficiency. This was a large undertaking, involving not only plant personnel but also university students, as many readings had to be taken simultaneously. The turbine had an overload capacity, allowing us to raise the output to 35 MW. We had the machine set for a test reading of 33 MW when Mr. Kirkland walked in from the control room and said to us, 'Boys, don't take the unit down until we advise you to because, at this moment, the city load is in excess of 100 MW.'

TRACKING POWER USE

In the 1950s, Edmonton used technology to streamline another process that had become difficult to manage due to population growth: billing. This was a giant step for a system that had been evolving very slowly since the utility's birth.

Forty-one employees produced about 39,000 bills each month in the early 1950s. This was a manageable number. But Edmonton was growing; 1,573,151 bills would have to be issued in 1965.

THREE PRONGS FOR SAFETY

"The two-prong receptacle for electric plugs, standard equipment in houses for years, is on its way out as far as kitchens are concerned," reported the *Edmonton Journal* in 1954. The Canadian Electrical Code called for the use of polarized (three-pronged) receptacles, which became mandatory in May 1954. These receptacles prevented many types of electrical accidents. Manufacturers began to turn out appliances such as toasters and irons with the three-pronged plug as standard equipment. This meant that people purchasing new appliances needed to update their household wiring.

William I. McFarland

William I. McFarland was superintendent of Rossdale for seven years, from 1945 to 1952.

According to an *Edmonton Journal* account, Mr. McFarland was born in New Brunswick, where he was educated as a teacher. After coming to Alberta, he enrolled at the University of Alberta and graduated in 1929 with an education that qualified him to work in the electrical industry. After working in Ontario for a few years, McFarland returned to Edmonton as an electrical engineer with the Light and Power Department. He worked for the street railway as electrical engineer and assistant superintendent until he was appointed power superintendent in October 1945. He later resigned to take a job with a consulting firm in Calgary. William Kirkland succeeded him.

Adapted from The Edmonton Journal, *1952*

The Price of Power

How much did electrical service cost Edmonton families? In 1952, the suburban domestic rate was $0.05 per kWh for the first 40 kWh. From 1936 until some time in 1957, a five-percent discount was given to encourage prompt payment of bills. This discount was eliminated in 1957, which brought in over $1 million in extra revenue. Telephone accounts were used to encourage payment after the discount was phased out; phones were easy to disconnect and reconnect without a service call.

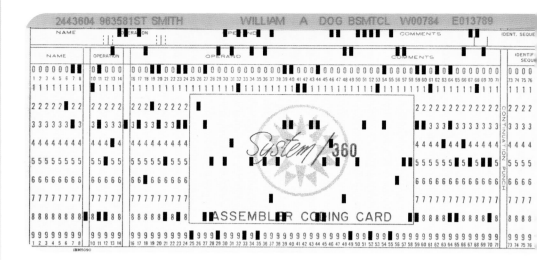

The utility responded by implementing a mechanical punchcard system, powered by a Remington Rand Univac computer, in August 1952.

Each customer account had its own punchcard indexed with a nine-digit number. An address and meter number was recorded on each card, along with information that a meter reader might find helpful (i.e., Is there a dog at the residence? Is it friendly? Is the house owner friendly?). Meter readers carried the punchcards with them as they made their rounds.

Working in the 1950s

According to George Faulder, working at the power plant in the 1950s required a range of different skills. "It was more hands-on involvement and [involved] a broader scope of work than it does now," he says.

We had a finger in every pie. When I first started in 1954 they put a lot of trust in a very young and inexperienced engineer. But I never screwed up anything big. Everyone worked together – there was a good camaraderie.

ABOVE: *A Univac punchcard for the account of a William Smith, who owned a dog.*

This camaraderie extended beyond normal working hours. According to Faulder, a social club began during the 1950s. The coffee canteen in the plant's machine shop financed the organization.

The social club held functions every Christmas at the Hotel Macdonald for all of the power plant employees. It was a dress-up affair, a formal gathering. There was a meal, then dancing to a band, and every employee was given a turkey.

The club also organized curling events for employees. This sense of friendship, as well as concern for one another in hard times, characterizes so many of the social and working associations of the utility's employees to this day.

New Poles

In 1953, the Electric Light Department attempted to make an improvement to the poles that held streetlights and transit system lines over city streets. The wooden poles that had long served this purpose lasted only about 30 years. Con-

EXPERIMENTAL USE OF WASTE OIL AS FUEL

In 1955, the City experimented with an alternative fuel for Rossdale's boilers – recycled automotive oil.

At present, the oil, dumped in the City's south side oil pit, creates a disposal problem. This was highlighted recently when the pit caught fire and sent heavy clouds of black smoke over the city ... The City is carrying out studies to see if it can be used in the power plant. Mr. Fisher [from the testing company] said he tested the oil in an Edmonton area plant using a crude oil burner and found it burned with "amazing" ease. He said it has a more intense heat than crude.

Source: The Edmonton Journal, *1955*

Edmonton's Electrical Distribution Department changed its late-night trouble service in the early 1950s. This change improved customer service and smoothed out employee relations. The system that had been in place since the late 1920s required that some employees work overtime; those employees received desirable overtime pay. Thus, on January 24, 1951, a 24-hour, seven-day-a-week trouble service was implemented. A dedicated staff inspected streetlights, responded to customer complaints, and did repairs that were difficult to do during the day.

Ed Carson worked on the trouble service shift from 1956 until his retirement in 1985. During this time, the utility experienced expansion, and Ed found himself working with a growing team of employees that he found to be "very dedicated." Ed also experienced adverse weather conditions that sometimes complicated his job.

My most frightening experience happened during a lightning storm in April 1956. I found a line on the side of a transformer burned. I went up the pole and with rubber gloves and bull cutters, I tried to clear it. As I was in the process of cutting, I touched a messenger cable and I was suddenly in the centre of a huge ball of fire. All the wires for two spans were burnt. There was a policeman below me, and two more a span away. They looked up the pole and saw me still alive! They were so scared they could hardly talk. I contacted the power plant and got permission from Bob McClary [former engineering manager] and the assistant superintendent to dump the circuit at the nearby substation so I could clear the de-energized line. I was then able to close the circuit back in and call for a line crew. My rubber gloves were badly shrunk up and the sleeves of my jacket were burned, along with a few eyelashes.

Source: Interview with Ed Carson

crete poles, though more expensive initially, seemed more cost-effective in the long term. Not only that, but they were also much neater in appearance. Thus, in December 1953, the completion of this changeover marked the end of wooden streetlighting poles for much of the city.

According to Art Baird, however, the concrete poles were not immune to structural degradation. They could be damaged, for example, when struck by vehicles, especially during severe temperature conditions in Edmonton's winters. The concrete poles were eventually replaced with the familiar metal 'davit' poles that bend gracefully over city roadways to hold lamps in place today.

A new type of lighting was also installed on some city streets. While incandescent lights remained in residential areas, mercury lighting was installed on principal thoroughfares in the downtown area. Mercury lamps provided twice the illumination of incandescent ones, but left people with pallid complexions. This, too, was a concern, and by the end of 1959, 12,407 "colour-improved," high-lumen, low-maintenance mercury lamps had been installed throughout the city.

FROM COAL TO GAS

The rising price of coal and the sudden abundance of oil and gas obliged the City of Edmonton to again consider switching the fuel of its coal-burning boilers to gas. The power plant was under continual pressure to reduce costs and air emissions.

All of the boilers at the Rossdale Plant burned natural gas by the end of 1955. It was reported that the plant was using about 7 billion cubic feet of natural gas yearly by 1958, at a cost of more than $1 million per year. Most of the gas came from Viking, and about 15 percent of the volume sales of the City's fuel gas supplier went to the Rossdale Plant to fire the boilers. The coal companies that once sustained the plant either closed their doors or found other contracts.

New Gas Turbines

It was forecast that yet another expansion of Rossdale's capacity would be needed by the late 1950s. It was then decided to add this capacity using gas turbine generators. These machines used jet-engine technology to produce power. A new building adjoining the west side of the Low Pressure Plant was constructed to house two 30-MW gas turbine generators, at that time the largest gas turbines in the world. Units 6 and 7 were commissioned in 1958 and 1959, respectively. The two gas turbines cost well over $2,875,000, and the building built to enclose them — the Gas Turbine House — cost $525,000. This expansion brought the utility's production capacity to 180 MW.

A short distance north of the Gas Turbine House, a new 72,000-V switchyard was also constructed. The switchyard tied all of the power output of the plant together, then sent it to transformers and substations throughout the city where it fanned out to every light bulb and electric socket in homes and industries.

A new control room was also necessary. This was built at the south end of the Gas Turbine House, and included $250,000 in panels, switches, instruments, and wires. It would not be long before this control room would also

TOP LEFT: *Construction of the new Gas Turbine House.*

TOP RIGHT: *The new gas turbines were assembled on site.*

MIDDLE: *The Gas Turbine House was built on the west side of the Rossdale plant.*

BOTTOM: *The 72-kV switchyard is visible in the foreground of this photograph; the completed Gas Turbine House is directly behind the switchyard.*

contain boiler controls and electrical panels to serve the High Pressure Plant in the sixties.

CINDERS OR NITROGEN OXIDES?

Soot and cinders, byproducts of coal burning, had dirtied everything from fresh laundry to ice rinks in Rossdale's vicinity for decades. City Council had been receiving letters of complaint for years. It was hoped that the complete conversion to gas in 1955 would alleviate this problem and bring an end to citizens' concerns.

Switching to gas did eliminate soot and fly ash from the boiler stacks. However, Rossdale's new gas turbines introduced a different type of pollution to city skies. Oxides of nitrogen (NOx), a byproduct of burning gas, now gave the air over Rossdale Power Plant a yellowish tinge. This haze was characteristic of gas turbines at the time.

The provincial health department moved to investigate the yellow smoke coming out of the Rossdale gas turbine stacks. Officials continued to insist that the smoke was harmless and non-sulphurous; they adjusted the temperature at which the gas turbines operated for further reductions. Further testing was required. This issue would remain unresolved until future decades.

DISTRIBUTION AND TRANSMISSION

While Frank Sinatra crooned and Elvis was rocking his way to the top with *Blue Suede Shoes,* members of the Distribution Department put on steel-toed boots and hard hats. It was time to find better ways to deliver electricity to the hotels and industrial plants that were popping up all over Edmonton. Demand was increasing, and improved technology seemed the only way to address the problem.

BELOW: *A redesigned distribution system allowed linemen to work on energized lines. Note the insulation wrapped around the conductive surfaces in this photo.*

By 1954, distribution voltage was increased to 4,160 V, up from 2,300 V. Substations featuring modern failsafes and designed for high voltages were built.

The utility's aerial distribution system was rebuilt starting in 1957. The new system included larger space clearances between electrified wires and non-energized components. This allowed "rubber glove hand contact" maintenance on energized conductors; previously, lines had to be de-energized when maintenance was done, which interrupted service. The new system allowed linemen to do repairs without interrupting service. The Alberta Government Electrical Protection Branch approved this practice in 1958.

In 1958, technological changes demanded higher voltage in the primary distribution line. This voltage was upgraded to 13,800 V after the installation of Namao Substation on 127 Avenue in north Edmonton. The Namao, Hardisty, Strathcona, and Woodcroft substations were designed to operate at 60/80 MVA, and were supplied by a transmission system operating at 72 kV. A substantial innovation was the use of oil-filled pipe-type (OFPT) cable, which operated at 72 kV and 60/80 MVA. OFPT cable carried current from Rossdale's 72 kV switchyard to Namao.

While the Namao substation was being designed and built, it was decided to operate an aerial transmission ring around the periphery of Edmonton to act as a standby for the substations.

Another First

Another distribution "first" followed quickly on the heels of the OFPT cable to Namao. An 850-foot OFPT cable was installed under the North Saskatchewan River. Encased in a concrete-covered pipe, the cable was installed the same way as the cable to Namao had been (*see Installation, page 57*), except it was buried in the riverbed rather than under a street. According to a November 2, 1957, *Edmonton Journal* report, the

cross-river electrical power pipeline is the first to be built in western Canada, and is the longest in Canada. A considerably shorter span is strung across the Don River at Toronto.

Back to Coal?

The use of coal again became an option as the decade came to a close. Gas prices had begun to rise, the demand for power continued to increase, and the City again needed to explore expansion. In 1958, building a new power plant on an altogether new site was considered. Calgary Power had built a plant at Wabamun, where coal was close at hand. It was unquestionably more cost-effective to build a plant near a coal mine than to transport fuel for long distances.

Genesee, not far from Wabamun, had

INSTALLATION OF OIL-FILLED PIPE-TYPE CABLE

The Light and Power Department, under the leadership of Superintendent Monaghan, used innovative new technology to build a transmission system capable of handling increased loads. One of the most significant new developments used in this new system was OFPT cable, which could carry previously unheard of amounts of electricity.

In April 1957, work was begun to install four miles of underground OFPT cable from Rossdale to the new Namao substation. An *Edmonton Journal* report of April 22, 1957 gives the details:

[The] first phase of the project will be to lay the cable along 104 St. underneath the east-west tracks near 105th Ave. Twelve-inch pipe will be drilled underneath the tracks from both sides, meeting in the middle. The 5 9/16-inch cable will then be placed through the casing pipe.

C.Z. Monaghan ... said that power should be flowing through the 72,000-volt line by next November. It will be capable of delivering 60,000 kilowatt-hours of power to the substation. The new system will tie in with the gas turbines being installed at the power plant. The cable to be laid this summer is the first step in a new distribution system for the city to provide about 30 miles of the new type cable laid at a cost of $2,500,000.

The cable is insulated with oil under 200 pounds pressure per square inch, the first time this type of cable has been used in Canada. Ultimately, there will be six substations, on the city's perimeter, similar to the Namao one, supplied with power by the new lines.

The present system, at 13,800 volts, becomes uneconomical to operate over a long distance because of the unwieldy size of the cable in relation to the power carried, and the relatively high proportion of power loss.

The OFPT cable installation process was fascinating. Lengths of 5 1/2-inch diameter pipe were laid down along 102 Street. A thin line was blown through each pipe; this line was used to pull a small cable through. This in turn was used to pull three high-tension cables through the pipe. The 2,000-foot pipe sections had to be spliced together and sealed.

Dry nitrogen was used to keep out air and moisture.

Public curiosity was piqued when transparent polyethylene tents began popping up along streets heading into north Edmonton. Set over manholes, these tents provided shelter from rain but permitted light to enter the manhole in which teams of expert line splicers were hard at work installing the OFPT cable. The art of line splicing was acquired through years of experience and training. Although it might have looked like a simple matter of wrapping tape around wire, it required considerable skill in obtaining the right tension, thickness, and number of wraps.

Once the splicing job was complete, high-grade oil was put through a purifying machine to remove moisture and gas, then pumped into the pipes. The oil used was very thin and manufactured especially for electrical insulation. This meant that more volts could be passed through the lines without risk of fire. Despite its ambitious scale, the cable installation project was completed two weeks ahead of schedule.

Source: The Edmonton Journal, *1956, 1957*

---

attracted the attention of City officials and the power plant superintendent. The Genesee site had rich deposits of economical and relatively clean-burning coal. Cooling water would be available from the North Saskatchewan River, and the site's proximity to Edmonton would keep the cost of transmission low relative to other mine-mouth sites. Consequently, coal leases were purchased in anticipation of the day when vast coal reserves would be needed to meet the City's demand for electrical power. Those days were fast approaching.

A NEW GARAGE IN 1959
The number of repairs that the Electric Light and Power Department needed to make to transformers, poles, relays, switches, circuit breakers, and other equipment grew along with the size of the utility's infrastructure. A garage and warehouse were needed to service such equipment. By 1955, the existing facilities were too small and outdated; a new building was clearly needed. However, Superintendent Monaghan had to

WES KNUTSON

Wes Knutson was chief engineer at Rossdale during the 1950s and 1960s. Wes was a most competent engineer, not only in the area of plant operations, but also in dealing with major plant expansions. The plant mechanical crew not only looked after maintenance, but also carried out turbine installation. Wes was in charge of all this work.

Knutson served on the British cruiser HMS *Sheffield* during World War II, and was in on that vessel's engagement of the *Bismarck*. Wes had a cutting wit, and never took himself too seriously. He was a very warm and colourful person. As a young mechanical engineer right out of school, I had a lot to learn from Wes.

The following incident tells a lot about Wes. It was 1955. We had just completed the installation of a large-diameter cooling water piping system that ran east from a new pumphouse. The day came when number 2 pumphouse was to be started for the first time. Things didn't go all that well ... someone reported that water was coming out of the ground between number 1 pumphouse and the turbine room. All attention turned to the spot, and sure enough, a leak of some nature was evident. We shut down the pump and arranged for a backhoe to dig the area.

After the pipe was exposed on top, [I] went [and] looked for the leak source. Be darned if it wasn't from a half-inch coupling that had been welded to the pipe to attach a pressure gauge used in testing the line. Someone had forgotten to place a plug in the coupling. While I was down in the hole, Wes was standing on the stairway platform at the end of the turbine room awaiting the verdict. [When I called my report to him,] he retorted back with his fist held high, "Faulder, your father wasted his money on your education!"

That incident was one of a number of memorable events that punctuated our days with Wes. Everyone held him in high esteem, and was always anticipating his colourful reactions in the course of conversation.

Told by George Faulder

LEFT: *Until the late 1950s, Edmonton's electrical utility used a small shed attached to the Rossdale plant for maintenance. This was replaced with a modern facility in 1959.*

present many arguments to the mayor and City commissioners to get a new garage.

According to a letter Superintendent Monaghan wrote to the mayor in 1955, the old garage had been made hopelessly inadequate by the utility's expanding infrastructure. The increase in the number of transformers and streetlamps illustrates this expansion. In 1945, there were 1,580 distribution transformers in service, which meant that approximately 100 transformers needed overhauling and repair every year. By 1950, the number of transformers in service had increased to 2,264, and by 1955 that number had climbed to 3,673. Of these, 800 required repair and testing every

Good afternoon, fellow citizens! Last Sunday, on my first broadcast of the new year, I reviewed briefly the outstanding events of 1954. It was an impressive year for the City of Edmonton in all respects – in sports, in industrial and commercial growth, in construction, and particularly in improvements and expansion of municipal services to fill the growing needs of our people.

As many of you know, Edmonton is the only city in Canada of comparable size where so many public utilities are municipally owned and operated.

This means that services can be provided at little more than cost, only allowing for operating expenses, taxes, and sinking funds for expansion and improvement.

Furthermore, results of profitable operations are used to provide more and better services and to reduce the burden of taxation.

Since these utilities are owned by the citizens, there is greater interest in their operation, resulting in better service for everyone.

Because our population continues to increase at a faster rate than any other city in the Dominion, greater demands are being made on the city's services than ever before. New residential and industrial districts are being developed which must be provided with public services.

...

Basic necessities of any modern city are power to turn the wheels of industry ... electricity to light homes and streets ... water for domestic and industrial use and for fire protection.

In Edmonton, these services originate in the municipally owned and operated power plant and water treatment station located at the north end of the 105th Street Bridge.

...

[In 1912,] the total value of the plant was just over one and a quarter million dollars, and the cost to the city of generating one kilowatt of power was about three cents.

Today, because of the use of less expensive fuel, automatic machinery and bigger units, this figure had been reduced to less than half a cent.

...

Today, capital investment in the plant is estimated at $6,700,000 and further extensive additions are even now underway or on the planning board.

Since the end of the war annual power sales have doubled every seven years, with recent indications that this rate is accelerating all the time.

...

Because revenue from operations is increasing by 12 to 15 percent annually, while operation costs are decreasing, the department is able to put aside appreciable sums each year for reserves out of which it will finance its own expansions as it has done in the past.

...

As part of the celebrations marking the city of Edmonton's golden anniversary last October, many of our municipal departments were opened to the public. In all cases this proved very successful and particularly at the power plant where the superintendent, William Kirkland, reports [that] more than 10,000 citizens toured the premises as well as the adjoining water treatment station.

Members of the staff were stationed throughout the plant to answer questions and offer information of interest. Pamphlets explaining operations were also prepared and distributed.

It was gratifying to note the interest expressed by our citizens who visited the plant.

From a CFRN radio broadcast made by William Hawrelak, dated January 9, 1955

---

year. Similarly, 2,621 streetlights were operated and maintained in 1945. By 1955, there were 7,500 streetlights to look after. Maintenance of the streetlights alone required both workspace and storage facilities. Spare parts for all of this work had to be on hand. At the time, however, equipment and supplies were stored at various locations around the city.

Monaghan got his wish. The Electric Light and Power Department moved into new facilities in early 1959. The new location, located at 108 Street and 121 Avenue, included a warehouse, shop, storage, and a garage.

The 1950s marked the beginning of renewed need for technological advancement and innovations within Edmonton's electric utility. New ideas, technologies, and demand increases pressured the utility to respond in ways that were progressive and met customer needs. In an almost breathless flurry of

DANGEROUS WORK

Edmonton's electrical utility continued to be reliable throughout the 1950s, in part because it effectively responded to population growth and technological change. The design of the distribution system ensured that faults could be compensated for; thus, service interruptions were rare and brief.

Occasionally, though, Mother Nature reminded the utility that she was really in charge. One weekend in early August 1958, a huge storm damaged power lines, toppled about 25 poles, and damaged at least two transformers. So many lines had been downed by falling trees and branches that customers were warned to watch for energized wires in their yards. The utility responded to over 2,500 reports of power disruption after the storm. Some households were without power for 24 hours.

The weather also took its toll on the utility's human assets. Lineman Waldemar (Goldie) Lehmann, aged 28, was toppled from a pole during the storm. He had climbed one pole adjacent to another that had fallen on a house. As he was disconnecting the damaged lines, the broken pole shifted, knocking over the one Lehmann was on. He received a broken arm and two broken ribs. He chuckles when he tells the story today, but he wasn't laughing when it happened!

Most on-the-job accidents in the 1950s were not fatal; however, a few took the lives of employees of both the power plant and the Light and Power Department. For example, a City Safety Department report reveals that between January 1956 and September 1958, three employees were killed on the job, a reminder that the utility's employees are always exposed to danger.

Source: Interviews and The Edmonton Journal, *1958*

expansion and addition of equipment, Rossdale Power Plant's peak capacity grew from 60 MW in 1950 to 180 MW in 1959. This would not be the last dramatic increase in capacity; future decades would see the utility grow even faster.

LEFT: *Meter maintenance at the North Service Centre.*

CHAPTER 7

Electricity Sparks the '60s

. . . . .

1960 – 1969

*T*he babies born in the postwar glow of the late 1940s came of age in the psychedelic 1960s. Many rejected conventional careers and values. Long hair, kaftans, love beads, and sandals identified this new generation. Driven by values other than material success, they wanted to shape Canadian society in fresh and exciting ways. One of their many concerns was the environment.

In 1964, Rachel Carson's controversial book *Silent Spring* was published. It focused on growing concerns about the environment and the effect of pesticides on wildlife. The book was a sign of the times – fewer people were willing to accept pollution as a necessary byproduct of industrial society. This was relevant to the Rossdale Power Plant, and Edmonton's electrical utility continued to find ways to reduce emissions.

Smog was not the only challenge facing the utility. The demand for electricity was expanding as a result of a booming economy, a growing population, and the utility's own promotional efforts. William Kirkland, superintendent of the power plant during the tumultuous 1960s, helped the utility meet many of these challenges. He oversaw the expansion of the Rossdale Power Plant and advised City Council about the best approach to take in building a new power plant on the city's outskirts, to expand the generation of power beyond the sturdy brick walls of Rossdale.

DEMAND INCREASES

Demand for power increased in the 1960s. Thanks to a postwar baby boom and an influx of people seeking work in the province's oil-fed industries, Edmonton's population reached 371,265 in

MILESTONES

1960
An OFPT cable using aluminum (rather than copper) conductors links Rossdale to Woodcroft Substation. This aluminum cable is the first of its kind to be used commercially in North America.

Power rates for domestic electrical power are $0.04 per kWh for 40 kWh, $0.02 for 110 kWh, and $0.015 for 150 kWh or more. The average consumption per domestic customer is 2,950 kWh.

By year's end, there are 36,496 electric ranges and 1,586 dryers in Edmonton.

1961
Edmonton annexes the town of Beverly, extending the eastern boundary of the city to 34 Street.

1962
Edmonton celebrates its first Klondike Days.

Canada launches a scientific satellite and becomes the third country in the world to launch a satellite.

1963
Power lines distributing power to new residential areas are installed underground, following a new City policy.

1964
There are 88,565 meters in service in Edmonton, and 28,425 electrical inspections are carried out.

ADVERTISING ON TELEVISION

For CFRN TV

Who says the good old pioneer days are gone forever! Man is constantly searching new horizons for better ways to live.

Take electricity, for example. Now *there's* a field of great potential! Discovered, yes, but not exploited to the fullest extent. Yesterday – an unharnessed element of nature, today – an energy we profit from both physically and economically. Look around your home, you'll find the advantages in every room.

Electricity for light, safe food storage, meal preparation, cleanliness, daily household chores, and many more conveniences. Some as-yet undiscovered. Scientific research is constantly exploring new ways to use electricity for an easier, more convenient way of life.

Your City of Edmonton Electrical System invites you to pioneer with progress. LIVE BETTER – ELECTRICALLY.

For CBXT TV

If you were forced to part with all but ONE electrical appliance, which would you keep: one of your kitchen appliances or one of your housekeeping appliances? It wouldn't be an easy decision, because you depend on ALL of them. Your City of Edmonton Electrical System invites you to LIVE BETTER – ELECTRICALLY.

Audio portions of television commercials prepared by Nattall & Maloney Ltd., advertising agency in the 1960s.

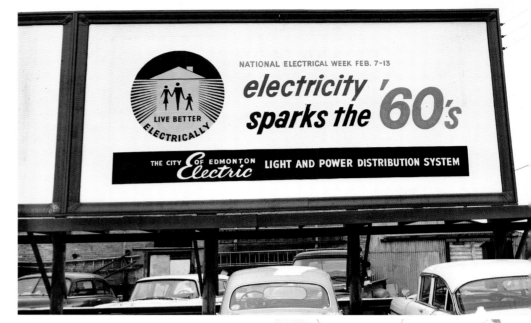

ABOVE RIGHT: *The City of Edmonton advertised the use of electrical appliances throughout the 1960s.*

1965, up from 209,353 in 1955. But there weren't just more people to buy power; people were buying more electricity than ever before.

The City of Edmonton aggressively marketed the consumption of electricity. Electricity was a profitable commodity the benefits of which were proclaimed on billboards emblazoned with the words "Live Better Electrically." This became a jingle that was broadcast on both television and radio. City-employed home economists advocated the use of electrical appliances.

These promotional efforts resulted in higher sales of electrical power. Between 1961 and 1969, domestic consumption of electricity increased by 5.5 percent yearly. Power sold to City departments would also rise – from 363,387,600 kWh in 1955 to 1,035,095,900 kWh in 1965.

City residents weren't the only customers drawing on Rossdale. In the 1960s, Edmonton's electrical utility and Calgary Power had an agreement whereby they paid fixed rates for emergency use of each other's generating facilities. Between 1960 and 1971, Calgary requested emergency aid 68 times and Edmonton made 26 requests for assistance.

EXPANSION

An expansion strategy involving both generation and distribution departments was developed to meet increasing demand. Rossdale was to be expanded once again. Plans were made to build an altogether new power plant. And four substations were built in the 1960s to deliver electricity to new suburban neighbourhoods via buried distribution lines.

Between 1960 and 1966, three generating units were purchased. Each unit was comprised of a turbine and a boiler that operated at higher steam pressures than the machines in the Low Pressure Plant could. These high pressure units were labelled numbers 8, 9, and 10. "Putting in number 8 was a real challenge," remembers George Faulder, a mechanical engineer at the plant between 1954 and 1966. "It was twice as big as the other units and operated at a higher pressure and temperature than the low-pressure turbines."

According to Faulder, there were other challenges as well:

In the Low Pressure Plant there were seven boilers in a row, feeding steam to a common header located at the rear of the boiler room. All the turbines took their steam from a common header. The consequence of that was that any boiler could supply steam to any turbine. In the high-pressure steam plant, one boiler supplied steam for one turbine.

To accommodate these large units, a west wing was added to the north end of the power plant. The High Pressure Plant was born. Its three turbines had a total generating capacity of 225,000 kW. Each of the new turbines used less fuel per kWh generated than the turbines in the Low Pressure Plant. The Low Pressure Plant contained five turbines with a total generating capacity of 120,000 kW.

ENVIRONMENTAL CONCERNS

When they were first installed in the 1950s, Rossdale's gas turbines seemed to be everything the City was looking for: their jet-engine technology offered quick-starting capability for peak loads. However, the limitations of this

BELOW: *Exhaust plumes from the short stacks over Rossdale.*

MILESTONES
(continued)

1965
This year, 1,573,151 electrical bills are produced.

1966
Rossdale's generating capacity reaches 405 MW, up from 225 kW in 1902.

Ninety-five percent of Alberta's farms have electrical power.

1967
The stacks above Rossdale's High Pressure Plant are elevated about 30 m to better disperse gas. Devices are installed in the plant's gas turbine stacks to reduce the formation of nitrogen oxides in the flue gases.

Canada celebrates its 100th birthday.

Workers installing a gas line near the Rossdale Power Plant unearth ancient human remains.

Edmonton's Provincial Museum of Alberta opens.

Work begins on the Clover Bar Generating Station.

1968
Ernest Manning retires from politics after 25 years.

1969
This year, 1,923,900 electrical bills are produced.

Apollo 11 lands on the moon on July 20. The spacecraft begins its voyage home on July 24.

SEWERS, STEERS, AND VEGETABLE GARDENS

A shaft for Edmonton's deep sewer system was being dug at Borden Park. In June of 1960, we were experiencing a heavy rainstorm that was to last three days. On the first day of rain, an accident happened in the sewer shaft at Borden Park. We were called out to provide temporary lighting in the shaft so doctors could perform emergency medical procedures. Upon arriving at the site, we found that the lighting was no longer required. We had a crew of eight linemen plus a truck driver and foreman. Our foreman decided we would take a tour of the north side of the city.

While travelling, us linemen rode in the back of the truck, in the "dog house." It was difficult to see outside, especially with the pouring rain. However, we were aware that the truck was speeding up. We peered through the lone window into the cab and found that we were chasing a steer down a muddy street. This steer had apparently escaped from the stockyards; our foreman had evidently decided that we should catch the animal. One of the crew decided he should lasso the steer. He took one of the ropes on the truck and made a lasso. He then stood on the back of the truck and prepared his throw. At this time another crewman decided to have a look; he was lassoed in error and nearly thrown off the truck. This was taking pace on the Rearson Estates, east of 82 Street, where the Yellowhead now exists. Many of the residents had two or three lots in which they grew vegetables. After avoiding the lasso, the steer decided to leave the street and stampede through these vegetable gardens. We left the truck to chase down the steer ... until a lady, furious at the destruction of her garden, chased after us.

We broke off our pursuit and returned to the service centre, where we were met by the general foreman. He asked where we had been; our foreman replied that we had answered a call to Borden Park. The general foreman said that he had received a complaint about a City crew chasing a steer through a woman's garden north of Borden Park. He was puzzled: who could it have been? Our foreman suggested that it must have been a telephone crew. It was agreed that this was possible. The call was deferred. Management is none the wiser to this day.

From notes submitted by
a utility lineman

INSPECTOR SAFETY

In the early 1960s, Edmonton's power utility had a terrible safety record. So a safety supervisor was appointed; he created safety rules. Many had trouble adapting to these rules; one employee had particularly bad luck with them. In the course of one week, he walked through a pane of glass beside an open door and broke his nose; then, while walking off a trailer, he missed the trailer's steps and broke his arm and collar-bone. This employee was in charge of enforcing safety for all field personnel! Today's safe environment was not achieved overnight!

As told to Lyn McCullough

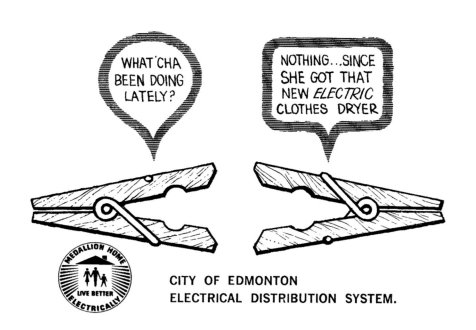

WHAT'CHA BEEN DOING LATELY?

NOTHING...SINCE SHE GOT THAT NEW *ELECTRIC* CLOTHES DRYER

CITY OF EDMONTON
ELECTRICAL DISTRIBUTION SYSTEM.

The Life of a Lineman

It all began when Gary Paul went to an job interview. It was 1963, and Paul was a lanky 19-year old with slicked-back hair, fresh out of high school and looking for a job. He responded to what he believed was a help-wanted ad for telephone workers (the telephone company was then City-owned). By the end of the interview, he was surprised to be offered a job as an apprentice lineman with the Electrical Distribution Department! Somehow, Paul had gotten his wires crossed and accidentally applied for work with the City's electric utility. Despite the surprise, he took the job and has never looked back.

Paul was fortunate to join the company when he did. In 1960, a new training scheme was developed by the utility in partnership with the provincial government's Apprenticeship Training Board. Electrical apprentices attended the Northern Alberta Institute of Technology (NAIT) as part of their training. "It was a four-year apprenticeship," says Paul. "I worked in the field and spent eight weeks a year in the classroom studying theory and doing lab training."

Linemen – then as now – were called upon to install, repair, and maintain power lines. The growth of new suburbs in the 1960s meant that this was demanding work. In 1963, the year that Paul began work as a lineman, 1,133 rotted poles were replaced, and an additional 68 poles were replaced as a result of car accidents.

ABOVE: *A lineman on a diving board.*

Although Paul was stationed at the North Service Centre, he was sent out on jobs across the city, often in sub-zero weather. Those were the days when crews travelled in an unheated "dog house" perched on the box of a flat-nosed International Truck.

Once a lineman was ready to start work on a line, he would strap steel spurs on his legs. He would shimmy up the pole by jamming the spurs into the wood and propelling himself upward. Once he reached the line, the lineman would lower a rope and haul up a "nose bag" full of equipment.

One of the most important items hauled up the pole was a "diving board." "We didn't have bucket trucks at that time," says Paul. "Diving boards were insulated planks that we chained to the poles and then stood on while we did work on the line." Other items included rubber line hose to slip over energized power lines.

The work could be uncomfortable and at times dangerous. Energized power lines have blown across Paul's feet. He has worked in temperatures so cold that sweat has frozen inside his thick rubber work gloves. But he wouldn't trade his job for any other. "I've worked with the best people I can imagine," he says. "This job has let me work in different parts of the city every day. It's never boring. I've been proud to be a part of this company."

With notes prepared by
Lyn McCullough

---

technology were becoming apparent in 1960, when nitrogen oxide, a potentially harmful product of combustion, seemed to be present in the exhaust of a turbine purchased in 1958. Mayor Roper maintained that the gas turbine produced emissions only when going "full out" to supply the emergency needs of Calgary Power. An unfortunate choice of words, considering that the gas turbines had cost the City substantial tax dollars. "Have the taxpayers of Edmonton been saddled with a $1,500,000 expenditure chiefly for the profit and convenience of the Calgary Power Company?" wondered editors at the *Edmonton Journal*. The troublesome turbine was eventually relegated to supplying power at emergency and peak periods only. The flame temperature in the turbine was also lowered, reducing the production of nitrogen oxide.

In 1964, new challenges arose. Now the emissions were coming from the silver stacks that towered above the new high-pressure wing. Staff at the generating station worked with the manufacturer of its turbines to find a way to burn fuel with fewer visible emissions. However, the problem persisted, and Alberta's health minister ordered the City to address its pollution problem by December 31, 1966.

City Council commissioned a $20,000 study to determine the composition of Rossdale's emissions. Joseph Lukacs, Dr. A. Rossano, and Dr. W. Oldham conduced 24 different tests from the roof of the generating plant. The results were not encouraging: the gas was being emitted at a rate of 90 to 200 parts per million. Safe concentrations ranged from 5 to 40 parts per million.

Meanwhile, City aldermen and Rossdale Superintendent Kirkland continued to argue that the pollution emerging from the stacks was quickly dispersed into the air and therefore posed no significant health threat. Consultants ultimately supported these arguments. City Council approved an extension of the exhaust stacks over Rossdale. The stacks over the Gas Turbine House were fitted with devices that helped to prevent the formation of nitrogen oxide.

BELOW: *In 1963, Distribution Department workers demonstrated the dangers of electrical short circuits. Over 2,000 people attended the demonstrations.*

THE ROAD TO CLOVER BAR

Edmonton had experienced growth in almost every decade of its history. Therefore, it seemed reasonable to forecast that Edmonton's population and its power consumption would continue to increase. Expanding the Rossdale Power Plant wasn't the only way to address this growing need. A companion plant, burning either coal or gas, at an altogether new site, was a possible alternative.

The Genesee area, located about 80 km southwest of Edmonton, had been first considered as a generating site in the 1950s. This site remained attractive in the 1960s. Test drilling indicated that the coal beds contained 45 million tons of coal with a heating value of approximately 7,800 BTU per pound, roughly equivalent to 3.8 billion gallons of oil. In 1961, Power Plant Superintendent Kirkland advised Edmonton City Council that coal reserves in the Genesee area made building a 1,500-MW coal-fired plant possible and economical.

Not everything about Genesee (or expansion in general) was right, however. First, coal-fired generating plants were expensive. Second, Calgary

LIVE BETTER ELECTRICALLY

In the 1960s, motorists on Stony Plain Road may have had their attention momentarily diverted by a gleaming display of modern appliances in the glassed-in verandah of 650 Substation. The display was part of Edmonton Electrical Distribution Department's promotion strategy – a strategy designed to attract the attention of female consumers.

In the 1960s, women were seen as decision-makers when it came to choosing from the more than 80 different household appliances then on the market. In 1962, the Electrical Distribution Department hired Rose Faryna, a home economist, to give advice to "questioning housewives" about the economical and efficient use of household appliances. From an office and auditorium (used for demonstrations and courses), Faryna provided interested groups with "tips on cooking, menu planning, laundry, and home management."

The faded green scrapbook created by the home service department in the 1960s contains clippings and photographs documenting Faryna's efforts, and those of her successors. It includes recipes for such dishes as "macaroni sauté" and "polka dot chili." Clippings chronicle cooking demonstrations with improbable new appliances such as an "infra red cooker." Thank-you cards from 4-H clubs, schools, and women's groups and associations indicate that Faryna's efforts were welcomed and appreciated.

While the work of the home service department may seem dated now, at the time it was part of an overall effort by Edmonton's Electrical Distribution Department to not only increase demand for electricity, but to educate the public. The utility's home economists actively promoted safe residential wiring. And while few of us would need to be instructed in the careful use of electrical appliances today, in the 1960s many still needed Faryna's advice. Home economists would continue to provide information to the public on behalf of Edmonton's electrical utilities until the late 1990s.

BELOW: *Modern electrical appliances were displayed in 650 Substation on Stony Plain Road.*

BOTTOM: *Rose Faryna, the Electrical Distribution Department's home economist, demonstrated appliances in this auditorium.*

A COMPETITIVE SPIRIT

Competition was in the blood of many Edmonton Power employees in the 1960s. "In the old days, they had a ball diamond at the North Service Centre," remembers Ron Donaldson, a former director of aerial distribution, now retired. Substation workers, meter readers, and waterworks employees formed teams and competed in tournaments.

Competition wasn't limited only to the ball field. In the 1960s, a small group of volunteers established one of Edmonton's most famous annual rivalries," says Walt Badowsky a former training supervisor.

We wanted something else to do, so one of us came up with the idea that we should get on the river and have a raft race. The plan at that time was to start in Devon. You'd go down there Friday night and build your raft from the wood on the riverbank and launch this thing and have a race to Groat Bridge.

The entry fee for the first raft race was a bottle of whisky, with the winner taking all. In the first year of competition, the prize was 12 bottles.

Badowsky recalls many hijinks among the competitors in the early raft races. "A guy named Andy Watson was pretty involved in the race," he says. "[The night before the competition] a few guys took a roll of guy wire and anchored one end to a tree. They reeled the wire out and tied it to the bottom of Andy's raft. Then they buried the exposed wire under the sand." When the starting gun was sounded the next morning, competitors scrambled to get their rafts out onto the water. Unfortunately for Watson, his raft managed to move out only a few yards before the wire prevented it from going any farther. "Everyone was on the verge of falling off the raft and Andy just thought he had run into a sandbar."

After a few years, organizers began to open the race to other groups, such

as workers from Edmonton Telephones. By 1966 a core group of volunteers registered the Sourdough Raft Race Association under the Alberta Societies Act. The race became an official Klondike Days event. Themes were established for the races. Rafts became more elaborate. "We've had two-person rafts, York boats, freighter rafts, and comedy floats," recalls Dave Walker, now director of systems development at EPCOR and a long-time volunteer with the race.

By the late '70s, over 100,000 people lined the river valley to watch the annual race. In 1979, over 200 floats participated in the event. What had once been a fun way to spend a weekend for a few utility employees had become an Edmonton institution. It's still one of the premier events during the Edmonton festival season.

With notes prepared by Lyn McCullough

Power was planning new, competing ventures. It embarked on a major expansion of its Wabamun plant, and hoped to build a hydro-electric plant on the Brazeau River within two or three years.

The Alberta Power Commission, a body that regulated the development of electrical utilities in Alberta, recommended that Edmonton delay building

LEFT: *Rossdale Central Control Room electrical board with John Simpson at the control board and John Hodgson in the foreground. The mimic board on the right was later moved to the North Service Centre.*

At about 3:00 AM on a cold February morning in 1969, technician Walt Badowsky was jarred awake by his ringing telephone. "It was Roy Fitzsimmons, the substation supervisor," says Badowsky. "He told me there was trouble on the system."

Fitzsimmons told Badowsky to get to the plant as quickly as he could. As a bleary-eyed Badowsky drove his truck down 109 Street, he was struck by the almost mystical darkness blanketing the city. Reaching the top of Walterdale Hill, his impression changed to one of wonder. In front of him were Alberta's legislature buildings, blazing with light. The legislature, powered by its own electrical generator, looked like a fairy castle. The buildings were covered in snow and bathed in a creamy yellow glow. A red clearance light shone from the tip of the dome like a cherry on a well-frosted cake.

After reaching the Rossdale Power Plant, Badowsky was immediately sent on to the Strathcona Substation, the source of the problem. The brick building was belching dark smoke into the cold night air. "The fire department was already there," says Badowsky. "They were spraying down the red-hot switch gear. Steam was everywhere." That was bad.

Badowsky finally persuaded the fire-fighters to stop spraying the electrical switch gear. Rubber and insulation on all the cables were burning. The station was shut down by remote control from the Rossdale Power Plant and the fire died down. A crew from the Distribution Department was left to clean up what remained of the Strathcona Substation.

The cause of the explosion was a deadly combination of water and electricity. Part of the substation had been under construction. Water from melting snow had dripped through an opening in the roof onto a circuit-breaker. The resulting explosion had a ricochet effect, knocking out breakers at the Rossdale Power Plant. Power was off for one hour in some parts of the city and fourteen in others. "I'll never forget it," says Walt Badowsky.

From interviews conducted by Debbie Culbertson

---

its Genesee plant and instead purchase power that it needed from Calgary Power. The power would come from Calgary's Wabamun plant, and eventually from the Brazeau development.

The Alberta Power Commission's recommendations did not sit well with the City. Mayor Elmer Roper declared that it was much cheaper for the City to produce its own power than to buy it from a privately owned company. Some Edmonton aldermen also argued that taxpayers of Alberta were unfairly subsidizing Calgary Power, which received interest-free loans, while the City of Edmonton received no such assistance.

Power Commission Chair James G. MacGregor countered these arguments by stating that Edmonton's proposed expansion would create an unnecessary and uneconomical duplication of services. "We want to get the three companies (Calgary Power, Canadian Utilities, and the City of Edmonton) to voluntarily look at this as if they were operated by one authority and as though they were one company," MacGregor told the *Edmonton Journal*. MacGregor said he felt that the companies should consider forming an independent generating company that would sell power to all the distribution networks.

This debate raised fears that the City would not get approval for its plans unless it submitted them within a short

RIGHT: *George Faulder, left, points out a steam jet air ejector on Rossdale number 8 steam turbine generator to a local journalist.*

OLDEST CURLING CLUB

The Edmonton Power Curling Club is the oldest curling club of its kind ... in Edmonton. The club was originally organized late in the curling season of 1945, [but] only succeeded in playing four games [that year]. In the 1946 season, however, the club got into high gear, with four teams entered in the schedule.

Very little is known about the [club's] first three years as no records were kept. The backbone of the club at the time was Nobby Clark, who always managed to come up with fantastic first place prizes, such as used meter dials and "antique lamps." All were very original and very hard to find.

Some of the prominent members at the time were: Dave Raitt, who was well known for his knock out game; Jack Torrance, who always played a draw game; and Bill Allan, who is still an active member of the club after 25 years.

Edmonton Power curled originally at the Granite and was [the Granite's] first ice renter on a regular basis. The club then moved to the Thistle for three years and finally to the Shamrock.

The Sangamo Cup came into existence in the 1949 – 1950 season, and was presented to the first place rink

of that year. Skip S.L. Clark, Third, J. Torrance, Second, N. Christophers, and Lead, H. Kinloch.

Two other trophies were added in the 1967 – 1968 season. The 1007 IBEW (International Brotherhood of Electrical Workers) trophy for the "A Section" winners and the Union 52 trophy for the "B Section" winners.

The skip whose name appears the most on the Sangamo trophy is Stan Hampton. Since he started dominating the winning circle it was obvious something had to be done. He was gently eased out of the Edmonton Power Department and up to the Commissioners Department.

Every skip's ambition to join the "8 Ender" Club became a reality for Norm Simmons and his rink, Tom Luchka, Howard Walsh, and Bob McClary on February 4, 1967. They also won the league trophy in the same year. Their success obviously got the better of them; the next season they won the booby prize.

The end of the 1969 – 1970 season saw Sam McGregor's rink emerge as winner of the Sangamo League Trophy and the "A Section" trophy.

From Watt's New, *October 1970.*

ABOVE: *Jim Curry, Wes Knutson, Pete Tuchsen and, in the doorway, Rudy Delmar overhaul turbine number 4 at Rossdale in 1969.*

Just as it seemed that the City was poised to move forward, a new proposal took the shine off the Genesee alternative. The Dynamic Power Corporation proposed that the City of Edmonton, Calgary Power, and Red Deer operate a thermal power plant on coal supplied by reserves at Ardley, 20 miles east of Red Deer. According to surveys, Ardley could produce twice the amount of coal needed for the economical operation of a generating station. Despite its initial promise, however, this proposal fell through when Calgary Power withdrew its support for the plant.

Initially, this power-sharing proposal seemed to offer the most economical solution. In a 1965 report, Power Plant Superintendent Kirkland recommended that the City consider building a power station adjacent to the Ardley coal field.

period. Despite this, the City took its time in exploring all possible options. Over the next three years, Plant Superintendent Kirkland would fill a special filing cabinet with estimates on future power requirements and potential options for meeting the City's power needs. It seemed that the City was

inching towards the Genesee alternative: by 1965, it had spent close to $250,000 on surveys and research at Genesee. Hopes were high that Edmonton could build a $50-million power plant at Genesee by 1969, with provisions for an additional $15-million expenditure on a later expansion.

WILLIAM D. KIRKLAND

William Kirkland was a fixture at the Rossdale Power Plant for almost 30 years. After graduating from the University of Alberta with a degree in electrical engineering in 1937, he worked for Toronto Hydro for eight years. In 1945 he returned to Edmonton and began his career at the City's power and water treatment plant as a draftsman and junior engineer. Kirkland became superintendent of Rossdale in 1952.

Having worked his way up in the utility, Kirkland had a special appreciation for those who were beginning their careers at the plant. "Bill Kirkland was extremely conscientious, responsible, and concerned about people," says George Faulder. Faulder says that Kirkland put a lot of trust in the small group of young and inexperienced engineers that were working at

the plant in the 1950s.

Others who knew him described Kirkland as a "hands-on" manager. During the search for a site for the new gas-fired plant, he wondered whether a site in the river valley flatland might be suitable. Henry Kasten, then a structural consultant with the utility, suggested that Kirkland take a look at the site himself. "It was mid-winter and the thought came to me that I had a snowmobile that could easily travel down the hill into the valley," recalls Kasten. "I suggested to Bill that I'd be pleased to take him on a reconnaissance trip on my snowmobile." Kirkland agreed to Kasten's offer.

On the appointed day, Kasten waited at the top of the hill with his snowmobile. When Kirkland arrived, Kasten was flabbergasted. "Bill had come straight from the office wearing

his dark-blue business suit, overcoat, gray fedora, driving gloves, and black oxfords with toe rubbers," says Kasten. "I, on the other hand, was wearing a parka and mukluks." Kasten nervously drove the power chief down the hill, all the while having visions of "rolling my client into deep snow." Fortunately, they had a good run down the hill and Kirkland quickly determined that the available area was far too small to accommodate a modern power plant.

Kirkland would soon oversee the building of the new Clover Bar Generating Station. When the water plant and power plant were separated in 1970, he became the general manager of the newly formed Edmonton Power, serving until his retirement in 1974. He died in 1985.

Sources: interviews and
The Edmonton Journal, *1985*

LEFT: *The North Service Centre was extended to house the Distribution Control Centre in the 1960s.*

However, the City was now considering a gas-fired plant. Gas fired plants were less expensive at that time. The Alberta Power Commission was concerned that there were not adequate fuel supplies for a gas plant, but this concern was addressed by subsidies. Frank Battistella, manager of engineering at the time, recalls highlights of the debate over fuel: "A federal government income tax rebate on gas-fired power generation ... lowered operating costs." Finally, a gas-powered plant would be a better "fit" for the load patterns of the 1960s. "The approximately 150-MW units in a gas-fired plant were more

BUILDING CLOVER BAR

Following City Council's approval of a new gas-fired power plant, a site had to be determined and ... purchased. We looked at four possible sites and finally narrowed it down to Clover Bar. The land was owned by two older women who lived in the New York area. They were contacted and the land was purchased for approximately $125,000.

The portion of the land next to the steep riverbank was the remainder of a worked-out gravel pit. The land was reclaimed ... and the initial plant layout was drawn up. Tenders were sent out for the building construction, the boiler, the turbine generator, switchyard equipment, transformers, and all the other components needed to run the plant.

Construction began early in 1968 and the first 165,000-kW unit was commissioned in August 1970. The erection of equipment was carried out by Edmonton Power personnel, with the assistance of supervisory representatives of Canadian and foreign suppliers. Edmonton Power staff acted as general contractors for the project. The building contractors were Smith Brothers and Wilson and Forest Construction Ltd. Kasten, Smith, and Eadie Ltd., assisted by Shawinegan Engineering Ltd., did the building design.

Frank Battistella was manager of engineering for Edmonton Generation, and later became production manager of Edmonton Power. He retired in 1984.

BUCKET TRUCKS, PLEASE!

The City of Edmonton greatly expanded its trolley bus system during the late 1950s and early 1960s. Trolley feeder lines were installed over dozens of city blocks and over uneven terrain around the river valley. The utility had no aerial lifts in those days; linemen used extension ladders to access the lines. We carried our three ladders over the total distance of the trolley line installation four times. Once on the ladder, we were relatively exposed to the hazards of electrocution. Can you imagine asking anyone to perform this today for $2.50 an hour? I can't.

However, because of jobs like this, the utility started to consider aerial lifts. We graduated from ladders to squirt booms — telescopic booms that were insulated. This led to the purchase of the first double-bucket insulated aerial truck in 1965. One such truck was purchased every year for the next few years. These units provided a much safer working environment for linemen; linemen could also be transported to work sites inside the trucks, where it was warm and dry. Today's personnel may take

these conveniences for granted, but in 1965 they were a great advance.

As told to
Lyn McCullough

suited to the demands of the 1960s; a coal-fired unit would be more economically sized in the 300 to 400 MW range," says Battistella.

Despite the foot dragging, City Council approved the building of a new gas-fired generating station in January 1966, and the government gave its go-ahead to the project. The Clover Bar site on the east side of the city was chosen to be the building site. By January 1968, the major pieces of equipment had been ordered, and in March of that same year, construction began on the plant.

As Canada entered its second century, Edmonton's electrical utility was an expanding utility with a growing infrastructure. It seemed that the utility was ready for any challenge. Few could have foreseen, however, the crisis that dominated the energy markets in the 1970s, when the price of gas rose dramatically and called the West's reliance on fossil fuels into question.

CHAPTER 8

A New Generation

. . . . .

1970 – 1979

$\mathcal{E}$dmonton gained much stature in the 1970s. The city successfully hosted an international sporting event – the Commonwealth Games – in 1978. The following year, it celebrated the 75th anniversary of its incorporation as a city. Much of its downtown core took on the form familiar to Edmontonians today, as many office towers rose to the skies. And its electrical utility remained the largest municipally owned generating operation in Canada.

The 1970s were not free of challenges, however. The energy crisis made a vital commodity both scarce and expensive. Motorists, manufacturers, and electrical utilities across North America experienced crises. Several strikes made operations at Edmonton's utility difficult. Despite this, the utility continued to grow – and to generate returns for the city.

CLOVER BAR

Gold-miner Henry Clover arrived in Edmonton in the summer of 1860. Clover had participated in the famous California Gold Rush of 1848. Now he wanted to seek his fortune in the waters of the North Saskatchewan River. Clover worked the sand and gravel bars near what is now known as Mill Creek, as well as a large bar further downriver. This became known as "Clover's Bar."

The generating station built near Henry Clover's claim inherited this name. By 1970, the first 165-MW unit was commissioned at Clover Bar. The fourth and final 165-MW unit at the Clover Bar Generating Station was commissioned in March 1979. This final installation brought the combined generating capacity of the Clover Bar and Rossdale generating stations to

MILESTONES

1970
The Electrical Distribution and Power Plant departments combine to form Edmonton Power.

Edmonton's water plant separates from Edmonton Power and becomes Edmonton Water and Sanitation.

Calgary Power's wartime debt to Edmonton Power is finally wiped out.

1971
Peter Lougheed becomes premier of Alberta.

Edmonton Power completes a city-wide switch from incandescent to more efficient mercury-vapour street lights.

The Province of Alberta passes an act that stipulates that the Energy Resources Conservation Board must approve of all changes to Alberta's electrical system.

1973
The oil-producing countries of the Middle East raise the price of oil.

1976
Edmonton's power plant operators strike.

1977
Tall steel poles designed to support high-voltage transmission lines make their debut in Edmonton. These are the first poles of their kind installed in Alberta.

TOP LEFT: *Clover Bar in 1973.*

TOP RIGHT: *A disassembled turbine at Clover Bar.*

ABOVE LEFT: *Inside Clover Bar; turbine number 3 is in the foreground.*

ABOVE RIGHT: *George Mitchell worked three months past his 65th birthday so he could say that he had worked at Edmonton Power for 40 years.*

FIRST IN NORTH AMERICA

Many cutting-edge innovations went into the design of Edmonton's Clover Bar Generating Station. One example is the "spring mattress" foundation table that supports the station's turbine-generators; it was the first of its kind to be installed in North America.

Clover Bar's turbine-generator units each have a common shaft that turns at 3,600 RPM. Due to tiny errors in alignment and balance, each of these revolutions sends a shock through the unit's supporting structure. Until Clover Bar, North American plants required that the supporting structure – called the pedestal – be several times heavier than the turbine-generator units. The pedestals were then able to absorb the shocks without subjecting the generating units to vibration. However, the pedestals had to be extremely massive, and thus took up valuable space.

At Clover Bar, a decision was made to purchase turbines from Escher Wyss Oerlikon of Switzerland. This company had developed a much smaller pedestal that included spaces for ancillary equipment. This was a desirable innovation.

This new pedestal used springs to absorb shock. The turbine-generator units rest on a heavy concrete slab, called a "table." A pedestal consisting of concrete posts and beams supports

ABOVE: *Detail from the "spring mattress."*

this table. Between the table and the pedestal, however, is a set of 126 specially designed springs. Thus, the pedestal, table, and springs offer uniformly stiff support, and are sufficiently elastic to absorb vibrations from the machine.

Clover Bar's spring-mounted foundation has operated successfully for over 30 years. Similar installations have since been used in Canada and other countries.

Adapted from text by Henry Kasten

1,050 MW. The two plants served a population of roughly 478,066.

The Clover Bar Generating Station quickly became the jewel in Edmonton Power's generating network. The plant produced power more efficiently and with less pollution than any previous Edmonton Power installation. As one engineer wrote,

Edmonton Power's Clover Bar Generat-

ing Station, environmentally speaking, is among the cleanest thermal plants on the North American continent. Because we use sulphur-free natural gas as a boiler fuel, the problems associated with pollution from sulphur dioxide are non-existent.

Learning from its experience at Rossdale in the 1960s, Edmonton Power also ensured that the plant's two stacks

MILESTONES
(continued)

1978
Edmonton hosts the Commonwealth Games. The symbol for the games, a blue and red maple leaf, is proudly emblazoned on the west side of the Rossdale Power Plant.

Edmonton Power field tests an automated meter-reading system.

The Edmonton local of the International Brotherhood of Electrical Workers goes on strike in July and August.

1979
Construction commences on the South Service Centre. As the city's land area grew in the 1970s, the location of a major service facility on each side of the river became a necessity in order to operate efficiently.

The fourth and final 165-MW unit at Edmonton's Clover Bar Generating Station is commissioned in March. This brings the utility's installed generating capacity to 1,050 MW.

Sulphur hexafluoride (SF_6) gas-insulated switchgear is used in Edmonton substations for the first time.

Edmonton Power has 186,115 customers, up from 175,249 in 1978.

Edmonton's 240-kV transmission system is expanded in the southern and western parts of the city using two underground oil-filled pipe-type cables.

An Explosive Situation

In times of stress, Edmonton Power employees used great creativity to solve dilemmas. They also witnessed incredible events. Willi Viehmann, a former shift engineer at the Rossdale Power Plant, recalls an incident that occurred in March, 1973:

In the early 1970s, the City of Edmonton's electrical load requirements were increasing rapidly and supply was provided from the ten units at Rossdale and the one unit at Clover Bar. At that time, turnover rates for employees were high. For that reason a great number of operating personnel within the two generating stations had limited service time and could not be considered fully experienced. In addition, generating units were operating continuously and some personnel had not experienced the shutdown and start-up of units.

Weekends were considered "easy shifts" because no maintenance personnel were on site, and shift personnel were concerned only with operational duties and some training. Such was the case on Saturday March 17, 1973.

Routine operating duties were carried out until approximately 10:00 when the lights dimmed in the power plants. This was followed immediately by the total loss of all generating units. No one on shift at Rossdale and perhaps at Clover Bar had ever experienced a total plant shutdown, so the entire city was without electrical power.

Operating personnel scrambled to cope with this unfamiliar situation. Back-up direct-current power (provided by batteries) was insufficient to allow safe and proper shutdown of the generating units. Hydrogen from the generators escaped into the turbine hall, setting up a potentially explosive situation. Start-up power from Clover Bar was unavailable, as the only unit at Clover Bar had also tripped. Communication with the distribution control operator confirmed that a fault had occurred at the Hardisty Substation which was severe enough to shut the system down.

Start-up power to the generating station was eventually provided by Calgary Power through a small tie transformer at Rossdale. Electrical power was first provided to the city shortly after noon; however, total restoration for the entire city took place late in the day.

Good cooperation between the generating and distribution sections resulted in a relatively short [power outage] when considering the severity of the failure and the limited resources of personnel.

This was the last time in the twentieth century that all of Edmonton was without power.

With notes prepared by Lyn McCullough

Good God, What Are We Going To Do?

We were about to start up Clover Bar for the first time. A group of commissioning engineers from the generator's manufacturing company were in attendance. One of them had a parcel under his arm: he pulled out this big bottle of alcohol and put it on the governor pedestal. At this time, of course, prohibition reigned at Edmonton Power: no drinking allowed. So we said, "Hey, we can't have that alcohol on site." "Oh," they replied, "we need this for the commission — we look at the meniscus to determine if the vibrations are okay on the turbine." Okay, we could accept that.

I've never ever had a turbine run up so smoothly in my life. They set it to Auto Run Up, pressed the button, and the thing started. At different speeds, while the temperature equalized, it synchronized itself – quite a feat. The engineers put a block load on the turbine, and it just sat there, because that was what it was supposed to do. But I don't know if they paid any attention to the meniscus.

When it was all done, they looked at me: I grinned and gave a "two-thumbs-up" gesture. What was I signalling? Next thing I knew, the top came off the bottle. The thought came to me: "Good God, what are we going to do?" But it was too late. They had passed the bottle around and drained it, as quick as that.

Al Pettican

RIGHT: *Danny Poleszchuk lighting off burners on number 1 boiler at Rossdale.*

BELOW RIGHT: *Edmonton hosted the Commonwealth Games in 1978. Edmonton Power constructed the electrical infrastructure needed to make the event a success.*

were tall enough to disperse pollutants adequately and keep ground-level concentrations low. Before construction began, tests were done to determine the existing levels of nitrogen oxides in the atmosphere. The results would later be compared with levels measured after the plant was fully functioning. Flue-gas recirculation equipment was installed to reduce nitrogen oxide emissions from the plant boilers.

From Promotion to Conservation

In 1973, the oil-producing countries of the Middle East raised the price of the oil they sold. It was the beginning of the "energy crisis." Between 1974 and 1980, the average cost of natural gas purchased by Edmonton Power rose from $0.195 cents per million BTUs to $1.207 cents. In 1976, the department took steps to keep costs down. Twenty-two percent of Edmonton's energy requirements were supplied through the Alberta Interconnected System (the provincial electricity grid); this electricity was cheaper than that generated using gas-fired units at Clover Bar or Rossdale.

No longer would Edmonton Power promote "living better electrically." Now the utility began advocating energy efficiency. Educational materials were developed to show people how to lower their energy costs. Even City Council got into the act. They established an energy conservation committee and studied ways to reduce energy consumption in the

buildings that City departments then occupied.

The provincial government scrambled to adjust to the new situation. It offered a rebate program to consumers who heated their homes with natural gas, but electricity consumers were offered only a partial rebate. The government announced that "the use of such a valuable fuel as natural gas for the generation of electricity is wasteful when other viable fuels are in plentiful supply."

Coal was back in vogue. In 1976, the provincial government introduced a policy that encouraged the use of coal as fuel. At this stage, the Clover Bar project was only partially complete. The City was committed to completing the project, however, because all the equipment had already been purchased.

BACK TO COAL

In the midst of the energy crisis, Edmonton Power's primary fuel source was gas. Generating costs were difficult to control. The utility turned to a plan it had considered several times in the past: a power plant on the coal fields of Genesee. With its own supply of fuel, the Genesee plant would be less subject to fluctuations in energy markets than its gas-fired siblings. And the Genesee Power Project would not just be a response to the energy crisis: Edmonton Power's managers had forecasted that demand for electricity would outstrip the supply from Rossdale and Clover Bar by 1981 or 1982.

With this forecast in hand, Edmonton City Council began exploring expansion options in the late 1970s. Edmonton Power could embark on expansion plans independently, or it could work cooperatively with such privately owned utilities

as Alberta Power or Calgary Power. The short-term advantages of cooperation were obvious; building the plant would involve a huge capital expenditure of at least $1 billion.

However, City Council was persuaded by the long-term benefits of an independent venture. Aldermen supporting sole ownership argued that a joint-ownership agreement would destroy the City's autonomy in managing the utility. They also argued that the new plant would provide greater revenues if owned by the City than if it was operated jointly.

Genesee was on a much greater scale than Edmonton Power's earlier projects. The proposed plant site would cover 3,000 acres, half of which would be devoted to a cooling pond. The plant

STRIKE!

For some Edmonton Power employees, the summer of 1978 was filled with more than backyard barbecues and camping trips. In the heat of July and August, Local 1007 of the International Brotherhood of Electrical Workers (IBEW) went on strike. For nearly two months, most of the electrical workers employed by the City of Edmonton walked the picket line. Two City departments were affected: Edmonton Power and Edmonton Telephones. Distribution and transmission workers, control operators, substation workers, truck drivers, and telephone linemen shouldered picket signs together.

According to Kelly Budge, then assistant business manager of the union, the main issue in the strike was wages. "The City was not prepared to pay an increase in wages equivalent to the cost of living," says Budge. With over 1,300 members, the union felt that it was in a good position to force the City to respond to its demands.

The timing couldn't have been better for a strike. In the summer of 1978, Edmonton was hosting the Commonwealth Games. Athletes and tourists from all over the world were flooding into the city to participate in and observe the events. And the games weren't the only attractions in town. The annual Klondike Days celebration brought thousands of visitors to the city. Leaders at Local 1007 knew that many eyes would be on Edmonton. How would the city cope if there was a power outage and its electrical workers weren't there to repower the city?

Ron Donaldson, then director of aerial distribution, was a member of the management negotiating team during the strike. Donaldson, like many Edmonton Power managers, had worked his way up in the department. A former power lineman, he had been "off the tools" for about ten years. Due to the strike, he and other managers had returned to the field, stringing power lines and laying cable.

"We worked 12 hours on and 12 hours off," remembers Donaldson. "We had no breaks and no weekends off. If there was trouble, I was sometimes called in." On one memorable occasion, Donaldson worked 48 hours straight, stopping only for a quick meal and a change of clothes. "We installed transformers, fixed cable failures, and even did some limited construction," says Donaldson. With only a skeleton crew, Edmonton Power rescheduled any non-essential maintenance work for 1979.

Meanwhile, on the picket line, the strikers were coping with challenges of their own. "We had electrical workers who worked on the trolley buses," says Budge. "And because transportation was important to the Commonwealth Games, we decided to picket the Westwood Bus Barns. On the first morning we were there, a guy from outside the city decided to drive his car straight at our picketers." Fortunately no one was hurt in the incident. However, the demoralizing experience would set the tone for the rest of the strike.

As the weeks passed, it was hard to tell which group was going to "blink"

first – Edmonton Power or the striking electrical workers. However, what may have been the deciding factor in the strike was beyond the control of both groups. The weather in July and August was warm and sunny. There were few electrical storms or other weather hazards that could have thrown the department's overtired and overworked managers into chaos. With no electrical crisis on the horizon, union leaders began to realize that Edmonton Power was not going to back down.

After seven weeks of picketing, members of Local 1007 held a vote to end the strike. The outcome reflected the ambivalent feelings of the workers. "There were only four or five votes more in favour of ending the strike," recalls Kelly Budge. "In the end we settled for only 0.1 or 0.2 percent more than what we had been offered at the beginning of the strike."

Although the workers lost the strike, Budge says that the experience was a powerful lesson for both union and management. "We learned that we had to find better ways to resolve problems," says Budge. "Although it took time, the union eventually developed a better relationship with Edmonton Power and we developed new forms of negotiation."

Those methods of negotiation must be working. The strike of 1978 remains the one and only strike by electrical workers in the history of Edmonton Power.

Source: Interview with Kelly Budge

would create more than 100 new jobs and generate millions of dollars of tax revenue for the County of Leduc. During the building of the proposed plant, 700 construction workers would also be employed.

OPPOSITION TO GENESEE

Progress on Genesee was halted a number of times as land owners, environmentalists, other power utilities, and the provincial government raised concerns about the new generating station.

Genesee-area farmers were among the first to protest the plant. Some of those whose farms would be purchased to make way for mining and plant construction wondered if they would receive fair prices for their land. Some long-term residents resisted moving – they didn't want to leave the farms that they had worked so hard to establish. Those farmers who expected to continue farming in the area near the plant wanted to know if their air would still be clean, and if water quality would be affected by the plant.

Environmentalists also raised concerns. In one newspaper, they argued that existing coal-burning power plants were "raining down on central Alberta a soup of heavy metals and organic compounds which may cause cancer and birth defects." Scientists at the University of Alberta also raised concerns about sulphur dioxide and its impact on soil. Groups like Save Tomorrow Oppose Pollution (STOP) and the Sierra Club of Alberta also challenged Edmonton Power and the provincial government to advocate conservation rather than build new power plants.

In 1978, the Genesee Agricultural Protection Society (GAPS) was formed. The group represented some of the people who would be affected by the proposed power plant. Group members lined the walls of Leduc County's council chambers and attended public meetings between Edmonton Power and local residents.

While some local residents were raising concerns about the proposed power plant at Genesee, other Alberta utilities were coming up with competing proposals. Alberta Power wanted the Energy Resources Conservation Board (ERCB) to approve construction of a 750-MW coal-fired power plant at Sheerness, near Hanna. The ERCB decided to hold back any approval until

DESCENT INTO THE VAULT

We meet the guys on 103 Street, just north of Jasper Avenue, west of the old Hudson's Bay store. The safety guy hands me a monkey suit, hard hat, and safety glasses. Says there are no ifs, ands, or buts – just put it all on. They all look at me like, well – seems like a woman in a vault is like a woman on a ship – bad luck ahead, no doubt about it.

I descend the steel ladder, thinking about all those old crypts I'd seen in European cathedrals. Dark, wet stones, but no bodies. Hopefully there are none in here.

Dale Grimoldby tells me that this 10-by-30-foot vault was built around '57, and originally may have had only two transformers in it. Today I see five transformers and a spidery maze of cables and tape. "So, what is all this stuff?" Dale points out with great affection which buildings each transformer services, and where each and every cable goes to. How does this guy know all this? "Twenty-nine years working for this company," he says, "and I'm one of only three or four in the company who knows how to splice cable."

My eyes are finally adjusting to the gloom. "What's all the black on the roof?" I see soot and burnt concrete above my head and on the wall. "Blew up," says Dale. "Yup, in '72, or was it '74? Anyway, one transformer blew up completely, another caught fire. Took us four days working 24 hours to fix the whole thing and get it back up and running. We put in all new cables, and got the mess untangled from previous installations."

Looks good to my inexperienced eyes.

"Everything okay down there?" says a voice from above. "No problem," says Dale. "Just taking one last look and a few pictures."

I climb the ladder into the mid-morning light. No chivalry here – the guys just let me climb out myself, no hand up. I turn in the suit, shake hands, thank the guys for showing me around, and head back to my office. As far as I know the vault is still there, transformers humming away beneath the feet of passing pedestrians. Only one thing has changed as far as I know, and that's the way I look at those heavy steel grates in the sidewalks around town. I know what's down there.

Told by Heather Marshall

A Clean Design

"It's the best damn looking power plant in North America," General Manager William Kirkland is reputed to have said about the Clover Bar plant. Like an industrial castle, the building has three five-storey towers. These towers house the plant's four boilers. These are connected to the centre tower by two wings that accommodate the administration offices and act as corridors to the turbine hall. The turbine hall houses the four turbines. A central control room overlooks the giant turbines.

White insulated steel panels coated in permanent baked-enamel curtain the steel girders that compose the building's frame. Floodlights shine down from extended parapets on the rooftops, accentuating the gleaming white walls. "The overall result was a fine-looking building that gave the impression of very clean operation," says Henry Kasten, a structural consultant for Edmonton Power during the design and building of Clover Bar.

From notes prepared by
Henry Kasten

BELOW: *The core construction team for units 3 and 4 at Clover Bar. Note the racks suspended from the ceiling: these held miles of cable.*

BOTTOM: *Clover Bar after completion.*

When is a house not a home? When it's a substation! Substations are distribution centres where electricity is transformed to lower voltages for distribution. In the first few decades of the twentieth century, substations had a capacity of up to 1,000 kVA. Today the largest substation has a capacity of 200 MVA (200,000 kVA). The equipment that distributes this power is housed in small buildings scattered throughout Edmonton.

"Substation buildings are designed to blend in with their local surroundings," says Art Baird, formerly of Edmonton Power. "Special finishing techniques are used so that they resemble the neighbourhood they're in." Modern substations may be disguised as suburban bungalows, dignified brick offices, or high-tech industrial buildings. Early substations were solidly built of utilitarian red brick. However, even in these early industrial buildings, white brick was used to create decorative geometric patterns on the front facings of the buildings.

The Garneau substation is a particularly outstanding example of sensitive substation design. In 1979, expansion at the University of Alberta and a residential and commercial building boom in the Garneau area was increasing demands on the distribution system. A substation had to be built. However, it would need to fit in with the brick and cedar homes that were popular in the university area. Following consultation with local residents and the city's Real Estate and Housing Department, the substation's name, exterior design, and landscaping were selected.

Choice of appropriate switchgear was also part of the design considerations. Sulphur hexafluoride (SF_6) gas-insulated switchgear was selected for the station because of its space-saving qualities. It required only 40 percent of the land needed by conventional switchgear and equipment was totally enclosed.

Today, few people passing the handsome building on 111 Street and 85 Avenue, which has been in service since 1982, even realize that it is an electrical substation. Its exterior blends in with the warm tones and materials used in many of the homes and apartments in the neighbourhood. The spruce and mountain ash trees planted in the late 1970s have matured and are kept trimmed and neat. The EPCOR sign is the only clue that the building is home not to a family but to the equipment that provides electricity to neighbourhood homes.

Source: Interview with Art Baird

TOP RIGHT: *An example of early substation design: 600 Substation on 124 Street.*

RIGHT: *The Garneau Substation.*

it debated the merits of Edmonton Power's proposals.

In July 1978, in a noisy meeting room at the Grove Motor Inn in Spruce Grove, Edmonton Power representatives placed an eight-volume application before members of the ERCB. Despite its length, the proposal was essentially a simple one. Edmonton Power wanted to construct and operate a 750-MW coal-fired generating station near Genesee. The application proposed that plant construction begin in 1981 with two 375-MW units coming into service in 1985 and 1986. Edmonton Power responded to questions about these proposals by stressing that the Genesee Power Project would produce electricity at less cost than any other new Alberta power project proposed or under construction. It was also pointed out that, unlike Alberta Power's proposed Sheerness plant, Genesee could be expanded into a four-unit station because of the extensive coalfields in the area.

Despite Edmonton Power's arguments, there was much to be said for Sheerness. Edmonton Power had run into community opposition to the project in Genesee, while Alberta Power seemed to be facing less opposition in the Hanna area. The County of Leduc had been swayed by local concerns to such an extent that it denied Edmonton's application for a development permit for the site. Premier Lougheed also expressed interest and support for the Sheerness project.

Calgary Power was represented at the ERCB hearings. In its five-page submission to the board, the company made it clear that it wanted a stake in whichever project the ERCB approved. The company came out in favour of Alberta Power's proposal as long as it could have extensive equity participation in Sheerness. The company also argued that if the ERCB did approve Genesee, then Genesee should be jointly owned.

For four of the seven days of the ERCB hearings, representatives of Edmonton Power were cross-examined about the social and environmental impact of its proposal, as well as technical and commercial matters. When the meeting was over, the ERCB decided to defer approval of the plant, although it did indicate that the Genesee project was satisfactory from a technical, conservation, environmental, cost-benefit, and social-impact point of view. The City rescheduled Genesee, and the department made plans to continue lobbying to have Genesee approved. As an interim measure to meet expanding demand, Edmonton Power arranged to purchase coal-fired power from Alberta Power for five to seven years from its Battle River Unit 5.

Edmonton Power gained an unexpected advocate in August 1978, when one of its former opponents decided to back

From pre-concept ...

Bill Kirkland had been very supportive of the Genesee concept years before anyone had seriously thought about it. He wanted the City to buy coal leases in the Genesee area, to secure the resources for the City. But the City wouldn't approve his request. So Bill, forward-thinker that he was, bought the leases anyway, with his own money – $20,000 – a huge amount of cash in those days. Eventually his hunch paid off; the City bought the coal leases from Bill ... for $20,000!

Lyn McCullough

to planning ...

Al Pettican saw Genesee through from conception to completion; he was the architect of the thing. During his first years at Edmonton Power, his ambition was to finish Clover Bar and move on – he didn't see any future at the City for a generation guy like himself, because they weren't planning new plants beyond Clover Bar.

One day in 1977, though, he was clearing out an office he'd just inherited when he found drawings of coal deposits in a field near Genesee's present location. At the time, Vic Kondrosky was general manager; Al went to him to ask for a budget to do a little bit of research into the field. Vic said, "No, we aren't going to waste money on that." Al wouldn't take no for an answer. He started to look into Genesee on his own time and on his own dime. "Back then," Al says, "we weren't allowed outside city limits in any City vehicle, so we had to put in the work in our spare time and go out to Genesee in my car to cook up

future plans."

Then Ed Kyte took over and things changed. Al's team had a budget then – $60,000 – to do the initial study.

Al's group presented its findings to City Council. Council asked the group to jump through some hoops, but, in the end, Genesee was built. So Al's extra time and effort paid off in the end.

Lyn McCullough

to design ...

There was a person on City Council who had always thought that we shouldn't be doing our own design work. He thought that we should be going to a consultant ... not just any consultant, but one consult-ant in particular. He was always trying to show us up with negative comments. One day, I was presenting the procedures for a particular contract to Council, and the councillor kept on and on with his ridicule. So I said: "It's all very well to make all these comments, but why not come and have a look at the way we're set up. If you still think we're incapable of doing our design work, then by all means, say what you want, but at least give us a chance – come and see us."

So he comes in to the office. We had a whole floor – about 125 to 130 people, all on that one floor. He looks at it, sees all the lines of people working – it was open-concept with rows and rows of people. They all had their heads down over plans, working away. He walks around the outside, looking at all this. Then he says, "Wow, this looks very impressive. How many people you got working here?" And, of course, I'm thinking, he's an engineer, he's devel-oped some sense of humour, so I say,

"Oh, about half of them." And that was it: from then on, every time I appeared in front of council, he made hay out of it. "Have you upped the average yet, from half those people working?" That went on for years. He went on to become a Liberal MLA!

Al Pettican

to contracting ...

I was in Chicago to meet with Sargent & Lundy, a firm we were considering to do engineering work on Genesee. We had the meeting in its offices, then went across the street to our hotel, the idea being that we were going to go in cars to a restaurant in the Hancock Tower for dinner.

A few of us got down to the lobby a bit early so, while we were waiting, Al Pettican and I stepped out onto the street just to look around, that sort of thing. One of the local engineers says, "Don't stand out there, it's not safe. You're in Chicago – don't take any chances, wait inside." Okay, fair enough. We waited inside and got ferried off to the restaurant, where we had a nice meal.

At the end of it all, one of the vice-presidents says, "How would you like to see a little bit more of the city?" We say, yes, of course. He took us to a "speakeasy" where we stayed 'til three or four in the morning. At that time, feeling none the worse for wear, we wandered down the street, back to our hotel, no fear, with nothing happening. We've laughed at this ever since – four o'clock in the morning is okay – six in the evening isn't!

Ken Warren

to public relations ...

The City had allocated a number of people to us to work in our public relations department during the Genesee planning stage. They were all very good PR people, too – for customers in the city, that is; they couldn't deal with the farm population. One fellow went to visit the farmers wearing tailored suits and shoes you could see your face in, which went over like a lead balloon. The farmers couldn't relate to the guy. He was more concerned with keeping his boots clean than he was about going into the houses and talking about cattle. The people out there had shut us off, even formed a group to oppose the project.

I was just starting, at that time, to build a house out in the Tofield area. I'd cut a little driveway into my property, and space just big enough to fit a tent trailer into and to get a little fire going. We'd been in there all of Saturday, my wife, the kids, and I, cutting down trees to make a bit more room, trying to decide where to build the house. At the end of the day, I was tired – I sat looking at the fire, feeling miserable because I'd been thinking about the Genesee issue. I needed dialogue with the people in the area, and they didn't want to talk. The kids knew I wasn't happy; they were tiptoeing around Dad, keeping out of his way, not a happy bunch.

Then Tony Vilcsak comes along in his truck, sees us, backs up, jumps out, chats with us for awhile, gets some willow trees, and shows the kids how to make whistles. In a while, he's got everybody organized, told us that his brother lives one lot down from us, and introduces us to them. He'd got us so comfortable

with him and things organized so fast that I figured he might be the ideal guy for rural public relations.

I asked him if he'd ever done any work like that. He says, "Yes, I ran my father-in-law's campaign when he ran for MLA in the BC government."

So, on Monday, I called him, had him up to my office, and offered him the job.

From there on, we had our work cut out for us but we were moving in the right direction. And, do you know how we got 'em on our side?

We were driving around one day, chatting with various farmers, when we came across Steve Lorincz, a local, in the field, lying under his tractor, trying to get it running. We were in Tony's truck, so we stopped and went over to have a look, saying, "What's the trouble, Steve?"

He said, "There's something wrong with the differential on this tractor – I can't move it to get it serviced."

Tony backed his truck in and opened the back – it was just like a mobile workshop, with trays of tools, jacks, and equipment, as anyone who knows Tony would expect. He pulls out a couple of pairs of overalls, we put them on, and spend eight hours working with this guy on his tractor. We released the differential, got it running, repacked it, put it together, and away he goes, cutting hay.

Within two weeks, Steve had formed an alternate Genesee association that all the farmers joined because they didn't like the fellow running the 'anti-Genesee' one. Within a few months, it became the dominant group in the area, and the other one – that was opposed to what we were doing – died out.

Al Pettican

the Genesee Power Plant Project. STOP announced at an August 6 meeting of the ERCB that it supported Edmonton Power's proposal. STOP president Paul McGaffey said that Edmonton Power was publicly owned and therefore accountable to the people it served. As a result, the City department would be more open to environmental concerns expressed by local citizens than might privately owned companies.

Despite this support, the decade came to a close without a resolution to the Genesee debate; it would continue into the next decade.

Edmonton Power profited from the efforts it made in the 1970s, though much of what it had begun would not be completed until the 1980s. Besides building an efficient new generating station, Edmonton Power developed strategies for coping with fuel shortages, which proved valuable in the coming decades.

CHAPTER 9

The Me Generation

. . . . .

1980 – 1989

OPPOSITE: *Desmond the Dragon, Edmonton Power's famous mascot, came to life in the 1980s. At left, Desmond smites a knight wielding a garbage-can lid.*

*T*he 1980s were challenging years for Edmonton Power. A natural disaster endangered its employees and ravaged its infrastructure. A new industrial regulatory system threatened its expansion plans. A slump in the economy meant decreasing profits. Through careful planning and rate adjustments, however, Edmonton Power persevered, and continued to supply revenues to City coffers.

GENESEE

Environmentalists, competitors, regulatory boards, and local citizens derailed the progress of Edmonton Power's $1.1-billion Genesee Power Plant project in the late 1970s. But Edmonton Power could not afford to delay construction for long; demand for power continued to rise and the utility had to ensure that it remained competitive.

In 1980, Edmonton Power representatives appeared in front of the Energy Resources Conservation Board (ERCB) to do battle on behalf of the Genesee project. Again, Genesee faced a competing project: Calgary Power had a new proposal on the block. It wanted to expand its new power plant in the Keephills area 16 km north of Genesee. Despite this, and despite continued opposition from environmentalists and some local farmers, the ERCB formally approved the construction and operation of the Genesee Power Plant in 1980. Detailed planning of the project began almost immediately, and site preparation started in February 1982. The targeted completion date for a first generating unit was 1987 and 1988 for a second one.

In 1983, foundation and steel frame construction began on the Genesee site, located 80 km southwest of Edmonton.

MILESTONES

1981
West Edmonton Mall opens; the mall expands throughout the 1980s.

1982
Edmonton becomes Canada's second-largest city by land area.

The City of Edmonton investigates the purchase of a gas-producing company.

1983
Edmonton hosts the World University Games.

Prime Minister Pierre Elliot Trudeau introduces the National Energy Program.

The Electrical Energy Marketing Agency (EEMA) is established.

1984
The Edmonton Oilers win the Stanley Cup.

The Edmonton Space and Science Centre opens.

Pope John Paul II visits Edmonton.

1986
Edmonton Power employees supply food hampers to 16 families during the Christmas season. The utility matches these donations.

CONCERN FOR THE ENVIRONMENT

Edmonton Power did not turn a blind eye to public concerns about the Genesee project. The Genesee Power Project Advisory Committee (GPPAC) was formed in 1981 to listen to residents' concerns and incorporate responses to those concerns in the Genesee planning process. The committee included representatives from the Genesee area, the County of Leduc, Edmonton Power, Fording Coal, and provincial government bodies.

Many residents were concerned about the strip-mining operation, which was Fording Coal's responsibility. GPPAC's efforts allowed Edmonton Power and Fording Coal to develop a mining and reclamation plan that removed only 300 to 500 hectares of land from agriculture at any time. Land was returned to an equal or better condition than it was in before mining. The time between mining and reclamation was to average six years. Land not being mined was to be used as community pasture. GPPAC was also responsible for the design of a new community hall in 1983, and the creation of a recreation area on the west shore of the "lake" formed by the cooling pond.

The generating station was built to address concerns about air pollution and other environmental issues. A state-of-the-art emission monitoring system aided operators who ensured that emissions were properly controlled. Edmonton Power's response to environmental concerns demonstrated its commitment to community needs.

ARTIFACTS UNCOVERED

While assessing the Genesee project area, archeologists discovered a very large number of pre-historic sites. Approximately 50,000 Native artifacts were uncovered; these specimens ranged in age from 250 to 12,000 years. The artifacts were collected by the provincial government and preserved at St. Stephen's College on the campus of the University of Alberta.

Source: The Edmonton Journal, *1982*

Following an internal review of the project schedule, commissioning dates were advanced to 1986 and 1987. By 1984 the powerhouse was complete and work on the cooling pond and switch-yard had begun.

Progress was not to be made for long. In late 1984, Alberta Power, backed by TransAlta Utilities (which had been called Calgary Power until 1981), applied to the ERCB to have Genesee delayed. In December 1984, *The Edmonton Journal* reported that "the ERCB ruled in favour of the private companies over the objections of Edmonton Power and recommended the start-up dates be delayed 18 months."

The private companies were concerned that the Genesee project's capital costs would increase power rates for all Alberta consumers. This was possible; in 1983, Edmonton Power became part of a provincial power pool. The Electrical Energy Marketing Agency (EEMA) purchased power from Alberta's utilities at a price that reflected production and transmission costs. The utilities then bought back the electricity. EEMA was created to ensure that all electrical consumers paid the same for their power, apart from local distribution costs.

The 18-month delay forced Edmonton Power to lay off 300 tradespeople and engineering consultants. Costs esca-

OPPOSITE TOP: *Bruce Cropley, a councilor for the County of Leduc, did the honours at a Genesee ground breaking ceremony in 1982.*

OPPOSITE MIDDLE: *Genesee under construction.*

OPPOSITE BOTTOM: *Genesee's extensive cooling and settling ponds.*

lated, perhaps at a rate of $7,000 per day.

When work resumed, the completion date for the first unit of Genesee was set at October 1989. Work progressed quickly. In 1987, boiler construction resumed, the chimney was constructed, the cooling pond was filled, and electrical installation had begun. As Edmonton Power's business was to produce and distribute electricity, it was necessary to find another company to mine the coal at Genesee. A joint-venture agreement was signed with Fording Coal Ltd. Fording began to produce coal in 1988.

In 1988, 500-kV transmission lines were built from the Keephills and Genesee plants to the Ellerslie substation. That substation's switchyard was energized to 240 kV, with a possibility that it would be operated at 500 kV at a later date. Finally, by July 1989, the first Genesee unit was operating at full load. Electricity generated at Genesee was commercially available through the Alberta Interconnected System by October that same year. The project had come in well within budget. By the early 1990s, Genesee was producing more electricity than any other plant operated by Edmonton Power.

RISING COSTS AND CITY GROWTH

The cost of natural gas rose throughout the early 1980s. Power rates rose accordingly. The average monthly electricity bill increased 12 percent in April 1981.

Edmonton Power gained 4,700 new customers in the following year, when the city's area doubled to 34,818 hectares. Despite this, 1982 was a financially difficult year for Edmonton Power

MILESTONES
(continued)

1987
A tornado kills 27 people in Edmonton.

1988
Wayne Gretzky marries Janet Jones.

1988
A 230-kV direct current transmission line links Canada's eastern and western power systems for the first time.

1989
Rossdale's Low Pressure Plant operates for the last time between August 22 and September 29.

due to a combination of poor economic growth and warm winters. Rising interest rates made financing more expensive. High gas prices continued. Thus, bills went up again in 1982, this time by 13.2 percent.

These rate increases complicated the introduction of Edmonton Power's new logo in 1982. A bright blue turbine symbol had been adopted because it was associated with electricity, and also because it symbolized the flow of electricity outward to customers from a central point. Public concern was roused when vehicles were repainted to incorporate the new logo. It was therefore decided that vehicles would be repainted only when it was necessary for other reasons.

The rate increases also obliged the

EDMONTON POWER SERVICE AREA IN 1984

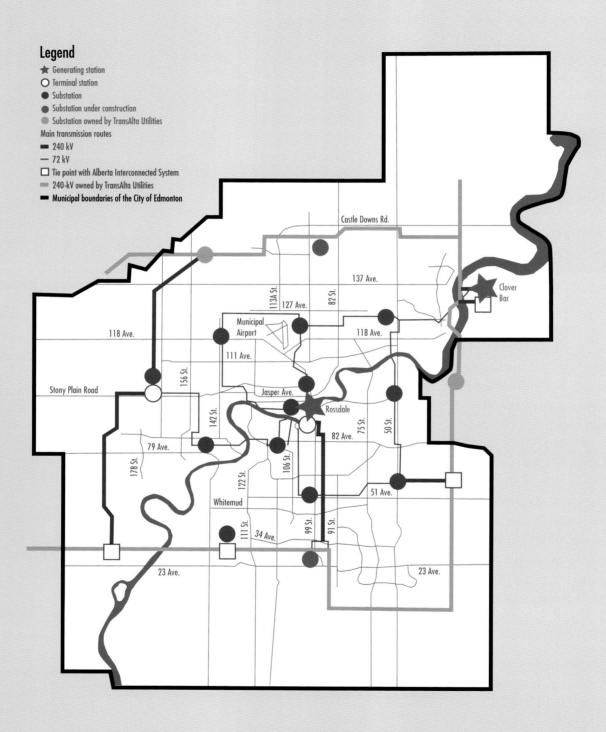

Legend

- ★ Generating station
- ○ Terminal station
- ● Substation
- ● Substation under construction
- ● Substation owned by TransAlta Utilities

Main transmission routes

- ▬ 240 kV
- ─ 72 kV
- □ Tie point with Alberta Interconnected System
- ▬ 240-kV owned by TransAlta Utilities
- ▬ Municipal boundaries of the City of Edmonton

Castle Downs Rd.

137 Ave.

113A St.

127 Ave.

82 St.

Clover Bar

118 Ave.

Municipal Airport

111 Ave.

118 Ave.

Stony Plain Road

156 St.

Jasper Ave.

Rossdale

142 St.

79 Ave.

178 St.

122 St.

106 St.

82 Ave.

75 St.

50 St.

51 Ave.

Whitemud

111 St.

34 Ave.

99 St.

91 St.

23 Ave.

23 Ave.

utility to cut costs in ways that did not sacrifice reliability. In 1981, a 240-kV transmission line around Edmonton was completed. The lines installed in 1981 connected the Jasper Terminal at 170 Street and 105 Avenue to the TransAlta Utilities substation in northwest Edmonton. The new lines allowed for more efficient use of the Clover Bar Generating Station, as existing 72-kV cables no longer limited the plant's output into the city. This cut costs because power from Clover Bar replaced more expensive energy from Rossdale. This transmission line would also provide for better distribution of electricity from Genesee.

In 1985, the Dome and Castle Downs 240-kV substations came into service, bringing the total number of substations to 35. Dome had fibre-optics for communications and included a new circuit-breaker system. In 1987 the Jasper 15-kV substation was expanded to incorporate 15-kV SF_6 breakers.

Also in 1987, TransAlta Utilities commissioned a 500-kV tie with BC Hydro. This created an electrical link from Alberta all the way down the West Coast to California. Edmonton Power could utilize this tie to improve system stability and to exchange energy.

Edmonton Power found ways to streamline its streetlight system. By 1987, 63,000 streetlights on Edmonton city streets had been converted from older mercury-vapour lamps to high-pressure sodium. Though the cost of replacing the bulbs was $120, each new

ABOVE RIGHT: *The South Service Centre opened in 1980, bringing 200 employees closer to customers in south Edmonton.*

RIGHT: *Linemen started to wear insulated suits in the 1980s.*

Ed Kyte

Born in Kentville, Nova Scotia, Ed Kyte was educated at Acadia University and the Technical University of Nova Scotia. Following his graduation, Kyte worked for Northern Telecom. There, he felt like a small cog in a big machine. So he came to Edmonton in 1967 looking for professional opportunity. He soon began working on the City of Edmonton electrical distribution system as a project engineer on substations.

Kyte thought he would work for three or four years to pay off his student loans, and then see where life took him. Marriage came in 1969, along with a promotion. He decided to stay with Edmonton Power. He made the right choice: promotions followed until 1977, when he became the general manager of Edmonton Power, the man in charge.

"[Being general manager is] a challenge," he said in an interview in 1991, "but I've thoroughly enjoyed it all the time." There were numerous challenges and changes during the years that Kyte was at the helm, including the long battle over Genesee. He led his team with confidence and resolve.

Kyte is quick to praise the employees he has worked with over the years, and is appreciative of the friendships that developed among them. Ed retired in 1993.

light saved about $29 in energy costs per year, so they would pay for themselves in less than five years. Additionally, they cast a pleasant golden glow rather than the bluish white light of the older lamps.

Computer technology greatly increased and improved in the 1980s. In 1988 the Supervisory Control and Data Acquisition System (SCADA) was put into operation, with hookups to the Alberta Interconnected System control centre. This allowed remote monitoring of transmission and distribution throughout Alberta. For the first time, operators had access to real-time information on capacity availability, load demands and system status; this enabled them to better respond to customer demand and to problems in the network. It was also conducive to proactive system planning.

PCBs

Public concern was raised over 240 sealed drums of toxic polychlorinated biphenyls (PCBs) stored at the downtown substation in the summer of 1983. A voltage regulator had ruptured some months before; the recovered PCBs and PCB-soaked rags were stored in drums at the substation until disposal could be arranged. People were concerned about further spills or leaks in this heavily populated area of the city.

Though amounts of PCBs in the gravel under the downtown substation were at levels below industry standards, the utility decided to move the barrels to a less-populated area in west Edmonton. After many unsuccessful attempts to find an acceptable site, another City

LEFT: *The core of a power-hungry city: downtown Edmonton in the 1980s.*

- A massive machine equipped with a 50-m^3 bucket lifts coal from Genesee's mine to a stockpile on the surface. This stockpile is subsequently transferred to the plant. A 450,000-tonne reserve stockpile is also maintained to provide a 45-day emergency supply.

- Trucks transport the coal to the plant, where it is dumped into an underground compartment. From there it is conveyed to a crusher. The crushed coal is fed into pulverizers that grind the coal to the consistency of fine talcum powder. The coal is now suitable for use as boiler fuel.

- In the boiler, a combustion chamber is pre-heated using eight giant blowtorches. These torches raise the temperature until it is sufficiently high to ignite the coal dust. This creates a continuous fireball. Ash is a byproduct of the burning process. Some of the ash falls to the bottom of the boiler where it is collected in a water-filled trough. This ash is removed for disposal in the mine. Other ash, called *fly ash,* is held by the flue gases from the boilers, and rises along with the gas. Flue gases are forced through an electrostatic precipitator, where the charged ash particles are attracted to a large grid. This ash is collected for use in cement production, or is disposed of in the mine.
  Each boiler consumes 230 tonnes of coal per hour. The stack is as tall as a 40-storey building.

- In the boilers, thermal energy heats pure water within the boiler tubes. The water boils and forms steam. The steam is then at a temperature of 538° C, and at a pressure of 16.9 megapascals.

- The steam is piped to the turbine. Nozzles direct the steam onto the turbine wheel blades, causing them to rotate at 3,600 RPM.

- The turbine shaft is bolted to the shaft of the generator rotor, which is a powerful electromagnet. Spinning the magnet within the stationary windings (wound wire) of the generator causes an alternating electric current to flow in these windings. The electricity produced flows out to the switchyard.

- In the switchyard, the voltage of the electricity is increased to 240 kV so it can be efficiently transmitted over long distances. The voltage is reduced by the distribution system before it is used by the consumer.

- After moving through the turbine, steam condenses to water in the condenser and is returned to the boilers. Water extracted from the cooling pond is used to condense the turbine exhaust steam.

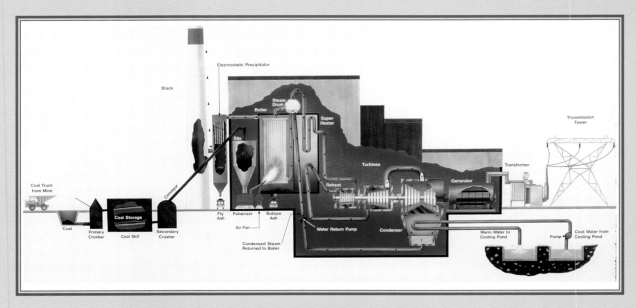

department, Edmonton Telephones, provided the location.

A metal building with an impervious paved floor was built. The building sat atop a dike, which was sealed where it met the structure's floor. Liquids stored in the building were kept in closed-top heavy-duty barrels, which sat in seamless containment trays. The building was monitored and alarmed for fire, and was inspected weekly. Provincial and federal environmental agencies licensed the building. The public was invited to tour the $12,000 facility upon its completion so they could see that the matter had been taken seriously and dealt with appropriately. By the decade's end, these hazardous chemicals had all been sent to Swan Hills Hazardous Waste Disposal Plant to be incinerated.

Edmonton Power commenced a long-term response to public concern over PCBs. The Network Decontamination Program involved replacing all PCBs with another type of oil that provided insulating properties similar to those of PCBs, but did not present the same hazards. During the 1980s, Edmonton Power became known for being voluntarily proactive on environmental issues, says Dave Walker, director of systems development at EPCOR.

PUBLIC EDUCATION

In 1985, Edmonton Power employees removed 187 kites from power lines. At the same time, per-capita power consumption rates were rapidly increasing. Edmonton Power responded to these problems with public education programs.

City safety officers visited schools to demonstrate the effects of electrocution. Wires from a high-voltage (4,000-V) hazard demonstrator were attached to a wiener. The wiener burst into flames, a reaction much less dramatic than the fate a child would suffer upon contact with high-voltage lines. The students were much impressed, and swore they would never fly their kites near power lines again!

Edmonton Power's home economist presented many power-saving innovations to consumers, including power-saver cords and vehicle block-heater timers. Customers enthusiastically embraced such devices. An expanded education program included teacher seminars, materials for primary school students, presentations on energy management and appliance purchasing, and customer consultations on energy use.

THE TORNADO

Late in the afternoon of July 31, 1987, the skies over Edmonton darkened as a funnel cloud developed south of the city. Disaster struck at around 3:00 PM. The funnel cloud, with winds reaching speeds of 416 km/h, touched down in southeast Edmonton, throwing vehicles, sheet metal, and trees into the air. The tornado released its final blast of fury over the Evergreen Trailer Park. In all, 27 people died as a result of the storm. Homes, businesses, vehicles, power lines, and poles were damaged.

The impact on Edmonton Power's infrastructure was considerable. More than one quarter of the utility's clientele, or 73,000 customers, were without power. A 240-kV transmission line in the eastern part of the city was completely down and the surrounding area was blacked out. Trees and debris short-circuited power lines. Transformer fuses were blown. Crews replaced 155 wooden poles and straightened and reset another 83. In addition, 36 distribution transformers were destroyed, 42.5 km of wire went down, and two 240-kV transmission towers were reduced to scrap metal. There was also some damage to the Clover Bar Generating Station, but

it was insufficient to halt production. The disaster caused a total of $2.3 million in damage to Edmonton Power property.

Employees from TransAlta, Alberta Power, and Edmonton Power, as well as numerous volunteers, worked together to repair the damage. The City of Calgary provided a 13-member work crew, Alberta Power sent materials, and TransAlta sent workers to get the system back into operation. In spite of the major damage, power outages lasted only between 20 minutes and 3 1/2 hours. By the Saturday morning, almost all of the affected area had its power back on. Nevertheless, employees working on adrenaline and long overtime shifts continued making repairs for weeks after. Some worked shifts as long as 48 hours straight.

Like most Edmontonians, Edmonton Power employees were deeply affected by the disaster. Seeing the destruction of trees and buildings is one thing; witnessing human tragedy is quite another. For those who were involved, the emotional

impact of the disaster remains to this day. Ron Donaldson has particularly vivid memories of the disaster:

I had taken my car to work that day because I was leaving right from work on holidays. I remember being in the control room and looking down at the hailstones bouncing off my Oldsmobile.

TOP LEFT: *Rushed repairs were made to Edmonton's electrical distribution system after the tornado.*

TOP RIGHT: *Jim Williams and Ed Kyte in the field after the tornado.*

ABOVE RIGHT: *The tornado flattened transmission towers.*

I heard on the radio what had happened. I couldn't get down the Yellowhead because of traffic, so I headed south where I actually met Doug McAvoy [substation director]. We couldn't move from there because of traffic and power lines, so we ended up helping the fire department and police look into vehicles that had been turned over in these parking lots. I will never forget it in my life. While we were doing that there was a county guy who was dead and they had pulled him out and covered him with a tarp. We were working but you couldn't keep your eyes off him. Soon we heard that the tornado had hit Evergreen Trailer Park. Someone came on the radio and said you would never believe it – everything is gone. He was hysterical. It looked like a war zone.

Clinton Keates, a troubleman for the utility, was touched personally by the disaster. He and three or four other employees were in the Evergreen area at the time the tornado hit. They weathered the storm in a bathroom in the South Service Station. When they emerged, they began to search for one trailer in particular: Clinton Keates' home. It was nowhere to be seen. Clinton, knowing that his wife would have been in the trailer when the tornado hit, was distraught. Yet nothing could be done. Employees started work on the cleanup and hoped for the best.

At about 4:00 in the morning, the Evergreen crew received a call for Clinton Keates. It was the Royal Alexandra Hospital. Clinton was nowhere to be found, so another employee went to the

TOP: *Linemen take a breather after the storm.*

LEFT: *The tornado stripped foliage from trees.*

hospital to see about Clinton's wife. He learned that the Keates trailer had been blown half a mile before coming back down. Miraculously, Mrs. Keates had survived, though she had been badly bruised. The employee was able to track down the Keates family and Clinton himself. The family had survived the ordeal.

The dramatic events of July 31, 1987 will not be forgotten. Edmonton Power employees can take pride not only in the prompt and efficient way they restored electricity to thousands, but also in the compassion they showed to people in extreme distress.

WORKING LIFE

Edmonton Power employees started a fitness club in 1982. After having their physical status appraised, 225 workers underwent a nine-week fitness program to see if they could improve their assessment.

Despite being physically fit, utility employees had higher than normal stress symptoms according to a survey conducted in the 1980s. In response, Edmonton Power introduced the Quality of Work Life and Stress Management program in 1986. The program was initiated to help employees deal with stress in the workplace. It allowed employees to address some of the issues that created stress, and to work with management to make changes necessary to reduce stress in the workplace.

DESMOND THE DRAGON

At the 1985 Grey Cup Parade in Vancouver, a giant green dragon made its first public appearance outside of Alberta. "Desmond," a giant lizard made of wire mesh, metal strapping, automotive

insulation, and fibreglass primer, was the brainchild of David Fraser, then director of substations and control. Fraser believed that Desmond would be a fun volunteer activity that would build camaraderie among workers and also promote the department.

"Dave did the original artwork and was the chief design consultant on Desmond," recalls Dave Walker. "Lots of people volunteered to work on the project. They spent about 2,000 hours building Desmond." By the time the dragon was complete, he had a tail and wings that moved up and down, and a nose that blew "smoke." He had an eight-inch-thick skin and could float on water. Using traditional Edmonton Power innovation, volunteers used an old washing machine transmission, hydraulic pistons, a 50-horsepower engine, and 24 fire extinguishers to create these impressive effects.

Between 1985 and 1998, Desmond participated in all Grey Cup parades as an ambassador for Edmonton Power and the City of Edmonton. He was transported by a crew of six to eight volunteers on a special trailer to games in Montreal, Calgary, Vancouver, Ottawa, Winnipeg, and Toronto. Desmond also appeared in the annual Sourdough Raft Race and in Yellowknife's Canada Day parade.

The only time that the fearless dragon appeared to be in peril was on a trip home from the United States in 1992. Desmond had participated in the Shriner's Parade in Billings, Montana. Edmonton Shriners had hoped that his presence in the parade would encourage the international organization to hold its next annual convention in Edmonton.

According to Dave Walker, American Customs stopped Desmond at the

ELECTRIC BLAST THROWS SOUTH SIDE MANHOLE COVER

A short circuit in electrical wiring under a south side intersection caused an explosion Wednesday, which threw a manhole cover into the air.

Heat created by contact between underground power cables sent flames and smoke billowing from the manhole at 99th Street and 52nd Avenue, about 4:50 PM, said Edmonton Power trouble lineman Jim McCrank.

"I was just sitting here serving customers and then there was a big explosion," said Dylan Parry, a cashier ...

"I looked over and the manhole cover was just coming back to earth and there was a big cloud of green smoke pouring out," he said.

Police arrived quickly but backed away when another blast of air from the manhole blew an officer's hat off his head, Parry said.

"After that they got a little more serious about it."

A police spokesman said a car was struck by the manhole cover, but Parry and other witnesses said the cover didn't hit anything.

McCrank said the cause wasn't known and added it caused only minor power interruptions.

From The Edmonton Journal, *1985*

border and demanded that his crew provide proof that the dragon had not been built or purchased in the United States. "That's when I started smoking again," says Dave Walker ruefully. "I was that

Hey, Buddy, Do You Have the Time?

In the early part of the twentieth century, electrical clocks would sometimes begin to run either too fast or too slow. But the clocks themselves weren't faulty; timepieces in perfect working order were as subject to this problem as any other. What, then, caused the problem?

Frequency instability was the culprit. Turbine generators tend to run at inconstant speeds; this causes the electricity they produce to change frequency. Thus, when a just a few generators are running in isolation, as was the case in Edmonton in the early part of the century, frequency can change considerably over time. This was remedied by maintaining the speed of generators, which was accomplished using an accurate clock.

Later, when Edmonton was connected to Calgary Power's generation grid, frequency stability was only a concern when that connection was severed. In the 1980s, subsequent ties linked Edmonton's grid to those of BC Hydro and a number of American utilities. Thus, the clock that once kept time for Edmonton still proudly hangs in Rossdale's boardroom, but is no longer needed.

Adapted from text prepared by
Paul Collis

RIGHT: *This is the clock once used to maintain frequency stability in Edmonton.*

worried that we weren't going to get Desmond back to Canada." Fortunately, Walker and his crew were able to convince American Customs that Desmond was 100-percent Canadian made. Officials finally waved the giant lizard across the Canadian border towards home.

In 1998, Desmond was retired. But old dragons never die; today, Desmond is in storage, waiting for the time when dragons like him are needed once again.

Edmonton Power would face unexpected challenges in the last decade of the century. These challenges would make it necessary to fundamentally change the way the utility operated. However, the progress the utility made in the 1980s enabled it to face these new difficulties with confidence.

ABOVE: *Desmond blasts his enemies with simulated smoke.*

CHAPTER 10

A Decade of Change

. . . . .

1990 – 1999

---

*T*he last decade of the twentieth century brought less technological change to Edmonton Power than previous decades had. However, it presented the utility with significant political and social challenges. A public debate over privatizing the utility raged in the media and at City Council. Further, the provincial electrical industry changed in fundamental ways.

While Edmonton Power could do little to respond to the privatization debate, it had to address the shifts in its industry if it wished to remain a viable entity. Thus, it completely reworked the way it operated. It could no longer appear or act like a municipal department. By the end of the decade, it had shed its old name, begun a process of rapid expansion, and investigated new ways to market electricity to customers. In short, it operated as a business competing in a difficult market.

RESTRUCTURING

The changes made to Alberta's electrical industry in the 1990s resulted from government efforts to alter its regulatory practices. Edmonton Power and other stakeholders had input into this restructuring process.

Under the system that prevailed in Alberta before restructuring, a company that wished to generate and sell electricity had to demonstrate that there was a need for new generating capacity — hence Edmonton Power's long struggle to win approval for Genesee. The provincial government regulated the generation, transmission, distribution, and retail sale of electricity. Alberta started a review of these policies in 1993; this resulted in the Electric Utilities Act of 1995, which called for a

MILESTONES

1990
The Edmonton Oilers win their fifth Stanley Cup in seven years.

1992
Jack Cressey is appointed chair of Edmonton Power (now Edmonton Power Authority). A board of directors is also appointed.

1993
Edmonton's new city hall opens.

David Foy replaces Ed Kyte as president and CEO of Edmonton Power Authority.

1994
Bob Phillips replaces the late Jack Cressey as chair of Edmonton Power.

1995
Bill Smith becomes mayor of Edmonton.

1998
Don Lowry is appointed Edmonton Power Authority's president and CEO.

1999
EPCOR buys 18,000 tonnes of emission reductions.

EPCOR begins selling natural gas.

EPCOR receives an award for its environmental initiatives.

ED KYTE
President and CEO
June 1977 – May 1993

Ed Kyte began his career with the Distribution Department in 1969. He became general manager of Edmonton Power in 1977, when it was still a city department. When Edmonton Power Authority was established in 1992, Ed became the first president of the emerging corporation, and served in that capacity until his retirement in 1993.

JACK CRESSEY
Chair
September 1992 – July 1994

Following City Council's decision in 1992 to create a Board of Authority as an interim step to full incorporation, A.J. (Jack) Cressey was appointed as Edmonton Power's first chair. A graduate in arts and law, Cressey had previously served in executive positions in a number of companies.

Unfortunately, Jack's dream for the company had to be passed on to others. Jack passed away following a cycling accident in July 1994.

restructuring of the electrical industry. Under the Electric Utilities Act, generation and retail of electricity would no longer be subject to government regulation, though transmission and distribution would be. Residential consumers would be free to choose a maker but not a distributor of electricity.

On January 1, 1996, the Electric Utilities Act created the Power Pool of Alberta. This pool differed from the one that had existed previously. The Power Pool of Alberta acted as an "electricity store"; generators offered blocks of power for sale and the pool matched them with retailers. The pool matched retail bids with the generators' price offers.

The new shape of the electrical industry had far-reaching implications for Edmonton Power: its customer base was no longer comprised of just its owners – the citizens of Edmonton. The utility would have to compete in a regional, national, and international marketplace. The former City department was reor-

ganized and changed its attitude about competition.

These changes were phased in during a long and complicated transitional period. First, the utility became Edmonton Power Authority. In 1992, a board of directors was established. The mayor sat on this board, though the City's primary role was to ensure that its interests were being protected. In 1995, Edmonton Power became a fully incorporated company, no longer a department of the City of Edmonton. Eventually, the mayor no longer sat on the board of directors, though City Council still approved annual business plans, budgets, and received quarterly updates.

Edmonton Power had a number of subsidiaries during this transitional period. Eltec was responsible for non-regulated activities such as streetlight maintenance. Edmonton Power was made responsible for water supply and distribution in the city; a subsidiary called Aqualta was created to operate the waterworks.

Another organizational change occurred in 1996, this time involving a complete change of name. A new corporate umbrella, EPCOR, was formed. All subsidiaries were now under this umbrella. Eventually, Aqualta became EPCOR Water Services Inc., and Eltec was renamed EPCOR Technologies Inc. EPCOR continued to be governed by a board of directors, and the City of Edmonton continued to be the sole shareholder. Encore Energy Solutions was formed, initially with other energy companies, to market electricity packages outside of Edmonton.

EPCOR was given a new logo and a new image a few years later. A news release issued on October 4, 1999 read:

New Look EPCOR Launches One Brand, Many Services

In a news conference with a definite customer focus, Don Lowry, president and CEO of EPCOR, today announced that effective immediately, Edmonton Power, Aqualta, and Eltec will all be known as EPCOR – a single, unified source for essential residential and commercial utility services.

EPCOR's Initial Public Offering, or IPO, in the summer of 1999 marked an important milestone in the company's transition to the private business community. EPCOR offered $150 million of long-term debt to private investors; the debt sold quickly. Brian Vaasjo, executive vice-president and chief financial officer at the time, remarked that the IPO was a "tremendous success," and credited

the obvious quality of the company's assets, strategies, and people. The organization absolutely impressed the financial community including both dealers and investors. This is yet another example of this company's ability to perform with the very best.

EXPANSION

Demand for electricity increased rapidly during the 1990s. To meet the demand, a second unit was installed at the Genesee Power Plant. On December 2, 1993, the new unit was synchronized with the Alberta Interconnected System for the first time, and was fired with coal on December 7. It began commercial operation in early 1994.

In the 1990s, EPCOR added to its gen-erating capacity by building new plants, with or without partners, and purchasing existing plants. Due to rapid demand growth and the newly competitive generating market, growth took place much faster than in previous decades. For example, in 1998, EPCOR entered into a joint venture with two other utilities to build a $320-million 416-MW co-generation plant in Joffre, Alberta. This became operational early in the new century.

PRIVATIZATION

EPCOR, in all its incarnations, had long provided the City of Edmonton with respectable returns. The utility was viewed by many Edmontonians as not just a source of revenue and a valuable asset, but also as a source of civic pride. However, in the new operating environment of the late 1990s, some Edmontonians began to question the City's involvement in the electrical industry. The regulatory protections that had insulated the City against risk were gone. EPCOR was competing in a free market, and was therefore subject to not only greater returns than before, but also greater risks. Additionally, the utility was worth a great deal of money; if it sold EPCOR, the City would not only protect itself from risk but would also experience a revenue windfall.

In an effort to come to a decision on whether or not to sell EPCOR, the City of Edmonton hired analysts from RBC Dominion Securities to assess whether or not it would be financially wise to proceed with the sale. The report concluded that EPCOR would be attractive to private investors, and that the City should sell it. According to Kevin Taft, an independent researcher, the RBC report was contradictory – telling the

SENIORS, LABOUR PROTEST SALE OF UTILITY

Citizens were mad as hell about the possible sale of EPCOR Thursday and said so loudly outside city hall, while council debated the future of the utility.

More than 100 protesters from senior citizen groups and labour organizations, as well as New Democrat MLA Raj Pannu, braved cold winds to tell council not to privatize EPCOR.

One senior carried a placard promising to "haunt" Mayor Bill Smith at election time should he support selling the utility.

Another protester bore a sign that said, "Keep EPCOR: Sell Bill Smith."

Many people took the possible sale of EPCOR personally, saying it would betray Edmontonians and leave them at the mercy of a faceless corporation that wasn't accountable to the public.

"To our generation, it's something we've built."

Many protesters called for a plebiscite, while others questioned the motives of councilors who supported privatization, accusing them of being too cozy with business.

"It would be selling off our heritage."

"This is the most valuable asset we have in this city and it belongs to its citizens. I find it strange that City Council should consider selling it without consulting citizens."

From The Edmonton Journal,
1999

TOP: *The cogeneration plant at Joffre, Alberta was a product of cooperation between EPCOR and other Alberta companies.*

ABOVE: *Edmonton Power added a generating unit to its Genesee Power Plant in the early 1990s.*

City that the utility was a risky business, while recommending to investors that EPCOR was a secure company with a wonderful long-term future.

Edmontonians protested the sale of EPCOR when the issue came to light. Many of them called the Citizen's Action Centre, a call centre that allowed people to voice their opinions. According to one report, within the first half of the year the Citizen's Action Centre received 251 calls from people who were against the sale, 59 from people who were looking for more information, and only two from people who were in favour of the sale. In one day, 189 calls were received, 172 of which were opposed to the sale. Meanwhile, the near-century- old municipally owned utility, which had committed itself to accepting whatever the public decided, sat tight and waited for an outcome.

Finally, after much public and internal debate, Edmonton City Council defeated a motion on Thursday July 15, 1999 to "have City administrators and EPCOR's board look at market interest for privatizing EPCOR." It was felt by many that too little was known about the restructuring of the electrical industry, and that a more cautious approach was in order.

ROSSDALE DEPOWERS

Much of the Rossdale Power Plant had become obsolete by the early 1990s. In 1992, Edmonton Power began the process of decommissioning the Low Pressure Plant and the Gas Turbine House. From 1992 to 1998, the two gas turbines, five steam turbines, and seven boilers were taken out of service and removed from the building. With the exception of three operational units,

Rossdale stood empty, waiting for decision makers to determine how best to use the building shell.

EPCOR wanted to make better use of one of the three existing units. It proposed the installation of a gas turbine. At least part of the Low Pressure Plant would have to be demolished to accommodate the new turbine; however, in addition to producing 170 MW of electrical power, the new turbine would

TOP, ABOVE and OVER: *Last looks: the Rossdale Low Pressure Plant was depowered in the 1990s, and its generating equipment was removed.*

produce exhaust gases hot enough to generate steam. This steam would operate number 8 steam turbine. EPCOR also wished to change the appearance of the High Pressure Plant so it would match the addition to the Low Pressure Plant building. City

In October 1993, David Foy joined Edmonton Power as its president and chief executive officer. Foy came to EPCOR with a broad background of experience, including three years as president and CEO of Phillips Cables, a leading manufacturer of wire and cable.

Council approved this plan near the end of 1999.

Once it was made public, the plan sparked a storm of controversy; citizens and environmental groups spoke out in opposition to EPCOR's proposal. Many felt that the historic Low Pressure Plant building was worthy of preservation. Others felt that the method of power generation was inappropriate. Once again, the electrical utility sought a way to respond in a way that addressed citizen's concerns.

The matter came to a close early in the new century. A number of significant archeological finds had been made on the Rossdale site, including the remains of an early Fort Edmonton and a burial ground. To many, these finds added weight to earlier arguments about Rossdale's historical significance. On October 17, 2001, the provincial government designated the Low Pressure Plant, the Administration Building, and number 1 pumphouse as historical resources. On October 25, EPCOR announced that it was no longer interested in repowering Rossdale.

DISTRIBUTION AND TRANSMISSION

EPCOR's distribution and transmission systems required renovation in order to take advantage of the latest technology, to improve efficiency, and thus to better serve the customer.

In 1993, the underground distribution system in the Westbrook (southwest Edmonton) area was completely rebuilt.

LEFT and OPPOSITE BOTTOM RIGHT:
Remnants of an early Fort Edmonton were discovered on the Rossdale site. The row of stumps shown are believed to be remains of a fort wall.

NEWSFLASH!

December 4, 1996

Power Crews Return from Lending Emergency Assistance
Stateside

Edmonton power crews returned home late Tuesday
night from Coeur d'Alene, Idaho, after pitching in
with emergency power restoration efforts. A series
of ice storms in Washington and Idaho caused such
severe damage that local power companies sent out
requests for assistance from neighbouring utilities,
including Edmonton Power.

"Given the severity of damage in the states of Washington and Idaho, with tens of thousands of people
without power, when the request for assistance came
we were pleased and proud to be able to respond,"
said David Foy, president and chief executive officer of Edmonton Power's parent company EPCOR.

Three aerial crews, one service crew plus a supervisor, totalling ten employees, were sent to the area
on Friday, November 22. Together they returned tired
but very proud of their efforts. "We worked with
crews from all over the northwestern United States
and some from British Columbia," stated Gary Paul,
supervisor of the crews in Idaho. "The weather continued to work against us, hampering efforts for the
longest time, but all of us persevered and the state
of emergency in Idaho has now been lifted."

"Pitching in to help other utilities in the face of
crisis is part of our business," commented Foy.
"Some of our crews remember the help that was needed
when the tornado struck just outside Edmonton, they
were eager to be there for others."

"Our crews are highly skilled and well trained for
emergency situations; this unfortunate circumstance
also provided them with the opportunity for hands-on
experience in an emergency situation," concluded Foy.

LEFT and OPPOSITE: EPCOR adopted news releases and other public relations strategies typical of large companies as it became a corporation.

This involved special tunnelling equipment and about 24,000 metres of cable. Edmonton Telephones and Videotron, a private company, assisted in the completion of the project; the general public also helped by enabling the utility to complete work without causing disruption to the community. Two main transformers that served downtown were also upgraded to handle 15 percent more capacity.

Throughout the decade, response to customer demand was both efficient and effective. By 1999, the utility was able to boast of 565 km of transmission lines (278 km aerial, 287 km underground) and 9,117 km of distribution lines. These lines provided services to 270,000 customers, 242,000 of which were residential and 28,000 commercial.

FOCUS ON THE ENVIRONMENT

The environmental movement was extremely influential in the 1990s. Society had become aware that it was producing huge amounts of garbage and air and water pollution, and that "greenhouse gases" could be causing the Earth's climate to change. Industries and consumers around the world found ways to save energy, reduce waste, and recycle what waste couldn't be eliminated. Environmentally friendly products appeared on store shelves.

In preceding decades, Edmonton's electrical utility had often taken steps to protect the environment. Starting in the 1990s, the utility advanced its leadership position in environmental matters with a number of new initiatives. One was the use of landfill gas (LFG) as a fuel in its boilers.

LFG is produced when organic wastes decompose in landfills. As organic wastes compose a large proportion of any landfill, a great deal of LFG is produced each year. The primary ingredient of LFG is methane gas, one of the more potent greenhouse gases. Burning LFG not only helps to conserve fossil fuels, it also converts methane into less damaging gases, and improves air quality near landfills.

Edmonton Power partnered with Environmental Technologies Inc. to develop an extraction and refining process for LFG. In 1992, the Clover Bar Landfill Gas Recovery and Treatment Plant was opened. A series of wells drilled into the landfill collected LFG, which was then conveyed to the treatment facility via a network of pipes. There, it was prepared for use as boiler fuel. Approximately 0.9 percent of Clover Bar's fuel is LFG. As of 1998, the project had recovered 93 million m³ of LFG from the landfill. In 1997 alone, sufficient LFG was recovered to meet the electrical needs of about 4,200 homes.

Edmonton Power published its first environmental policy in 1992. This policy expressed a commitment to environmentally sensitive and efficient approaches to power production that responded to public concerns.

This new policy would provide a backdrop for the various programs Edmonton Power and EPCOR developed and implemented over the remainder of the decade. Not only would the company comply with legal limits placed on emissions, it set goals to

ANOTHER FIRST!

October 25, 1999

TRADING PROCESS PROMOTES CARBON DIOXIDE REDUCTIONS
In keeping with its commitment to help Canada meet its carbon dioxide reduction targets, EPCOR Utilities Inc. announced that it has completed the world's first carbon dioxide trade conducted through a commodity exchange.

EPCOR purchased 18,000 tonnes of emission reductions from TransAlta Utilities through the newly formed, Alberta-based KEFI Exchange. The 18,000 tonnes of carbon dioxide represented in the trade is equal to the annual emissions of about 3,000 automobiles.

"The fact that EPCOR and TransAlta have come forward to make the deal demonstrates their commitment to helping create innovative, market-based approaches to managing greenhouse gas emissions," says Sheldon Fulton, president of KEFI Exchange.

For EPCOR, emission trading represents just one element of an integrated climate change program, which also includes:
* Commitment to renewable and alternate energy (i.e., landfill gas, solar, small hydro projects)
* Energy efficiency at our generating stations
* Working with our customers to reduce energy consumption
* Carbon sequestration (i.e., using trees and soils to capture carbon dioxide from the air)

This emission trade would be the first of several. Look for further discussion on this topic in the Afterword.

exceed government expectations. In fact, environmental concern would be a large factor in the company's response to restructuring as the century came to a close.

In 1993, as Edmonton Power was

"getting its feet wet" with its new environment policy, some very practical, customer-related activities were undertaken. One of these was the "Old Fridge Roundup." Three thousand, three hundred and eighty four used fridges and

Rob Phillips
Chair
November 1994 – December 1998

In November of 1994, City Council appointed Bob Phillips as chair of EPCOR. Educated in engineering and law, Phillips had previously served a number of large corporations, including Husky Oil, as vice-president. He was also a Trustee of the Canadian Parks and Wilderness Society.

Phillips is a strong supporter of life-long learning. "It's something I believe in and something I've instilled in my children. People may look at my background and say, 'This guy changes jobs a lot; he must get bored easily,' but that's not it. I like new challenges, new things to learn." And that is how he saw his work with EPCOR.

Phillips was born and raised in Edmonton. He and his wife and two children now reside in British Columbia.

LEFT: *A group of scouts tours the Genesee Power Plant in the 1990s.*

freezers were collected from individuals, and from these 918 kg of chloro-fluoro-carbons (CFCs) were recovered, along with 382 tonnes of recycled metal. This was beneficial because CFCs contribute to the destruction of the ozone layer, and the estimated future savings in electricity use came to nearly 3.9 million kWh per year.

The PCB elimination program continued with the removal or decontamination of 208 transformers and 33 capacitors in 1993. By 1999, after testing 2,774 transformers, only 37 contained PCB concentrations higher than 150 parts per million (PPM). Government regulations allow 200 PPM, while EPCOR's standard is 150 PPM. Contaminated oil from these 37

EPCOR AND NATURAL GAS

By the end of the twentieth century, EPCOR had been a consumer of natural gas for decades: many of its burners used the fuel. But in October 1999, the utility also became a supplier of natural gas when it began offering the fuel to industrial and commercial customers. Then, in December of the same year, EPCOR purchased Alberta Natural Gas Savings Corporation (ANGSC) and gained access to that company's customer base of 30,000 residential consumers.

transformers was disposed of at the Swan Hills Waste Treatment Facility.

In 1997, the Canadian government agreed to follow the terms of the Kyoto Protocol, which committed the country to reduce its greenhouse gas emissions by 6 percent of 1990 levels. This posed a major challenge to fossil fuel-based industries such as EPCOR. Carbon dioxide (CO_2), which is emitted when fossil fuels are burned, is one of the main contributors to greenhouse gases. Consequently, Rossdale, Clover Bar, and Genesee needed to be assessed in terms of the possibilities for further cost-effective emissions reductions.

As a step toward meeting the Kyoto target, EPCOR voluntarily committed itself to reduce its CO_2 emissions by one million tonnes annually by the year 2000. To achieve this, generating stations were made more efficient, landfill gas use was increased, wooden poles were recycled, trees were planted, and solar electric generation was introduced. The combined efforts of numerous programs allowed the company to state "our overall

DON LOWRY
President and CEO
February 1998 – present

As past chair of Alta Telecom Inc. and the president and chief operating officer of Telus Communications Inc., Lowry came to EPCOR with a strong background in leading companies through the transitions of a restructuring market. When he accepted his new position, he was quoted as saying:

I am impressed with the many accomplishments that EPCOR and its subsidiaries have achieved over the past few years. I look forward to working with the EPCOR team as together we face the challenges of [restructuring].

Lowry, his wife, and their two children live in Edmonton.

HUGH BOLTON
Chair
January 2000 – present

In January 2000, Edmonton City Council appointed Hugh Bolton as EPCOR's third chair of the board. Bolton is a respected senior business executive who recently retired from Pricewaterhouse-Coopers in Toronto, where he had a six-year term as chair and chief executive partner of Coopers and Lybrand Canada.

Bolton has a wealth of senior domestic and international business experience. His experience is particularly valuable as EPCOR expands its customer base beyond Edmonton's city limits, beyond the provincial boundaries, and into the North American market.

SOLAR POWER TOPS THE EPCOR TOWER

Have you ever wondered what is on top of the glass, steel, and concrete towers that loom over Jasper Avenue, Edmonton's main downtown artery? Probably not. But if you entered EPCOR Centre and took the elevator all the way up to the rooftop, you'd be in for a bit of a surprise. There, basking in the sun every day of the year, is a series of photovoltaic cells that provide 13 kW of power to the Power Pool of Alberta. Not only does this system produce power to EPCOR's Green Power program, it also provides heating, ventilation, and air-conditioning savings to the building by shading the roof in summer and providing between R15 and R20 insulation in the winter.

When it was installed in November 1996, the system achieved some milestones for building-integrated photovoltaics (BIPV):

- It was the highest elevation BIPV project ever mounted on a building;

- It was the largest BIPV project in Canada, and the third-largest photovoltaic system in Canada.

EPCOR's BIPV project was a successful – and profitable – venture.

ABOVE: *The solar array atop EPCOR's corporate offices in downtown Edmonton.*

RIGHT: *The solar array under construction in November, 1996.*

I ♥ Green Power

program of reductions and offsets now totals 1,149,800 tonnes per year to be delivered in 2000." Not only had EPCOR reached its goal, it had exceeded it.

The International Standards Organization (ISO) wished to encourage companies to work on their environmental performance. It established an internationally recognized environmental standard called ISO 14001. Compliance with these standards is voluntary. In 2000 EPCOR became the first utility in Canada to have all of its generating plants meet ISO 14001 standards; distribution and transmission operations became registered in 2001.

The late 1990s also brought about the introduction of the Green Power Program. This allowed customers to purchase energy from such sources as solar, wind, small hydro, and biomass (wood wastes) combustion for $10 to

PEREGRINES AT GENESEE

The fastest animal on the planet – and one of Canada's most endangered species – has flourished at Genesee for more than a decade.

The peregrine falcon has never been common; populations are naturally sparse because a breeding couple will jealously defend a large territory. However, the birds were once found in every part of Canada except a few high Arctic islands and Newfoundland; its range also extended south to the United States-Mexico border. Unfortunately, they vanished from most of this range in the mid-twentieth century, victims of DDT, a pesticide used in agriculture. By the late 1960s, peregrines could no longer be found in most of southern Canada; the species was listed as endangered in 1971.

Bob Joyes, a maintenance foreman at EPCOR's Genesee plant, suspects that peregrines first began nesting at the station in 1989. That's when staff first noted nests built near the station's fresh air intake. It wasn't until 1993 that a security guard positively identified the raptor's distinctive markings.

It is not a complete surprise that the birds choose a generating station as a place to raise their young year after year. The air intake is well protected from the elements and is hidden from view. Another draw could be the plant's cooling ponds; gulls, ducks, and pigeons, all peregrine prey, live around the water's edge. Bob Joyes has watched the birds hunt in pairs: one bird flushes out the prey, and the other swoops in from a hiding place to kill the unsuspecting victim.

After discovering the raptors in their midst, Genesee staff installed an expertly designed nesting box on the plant's giant smoke stack. From this vantage point, the birds had an excellent view of their hunting grounds, and could raise their young in seclusion. Joyes speculated that as many as three or four chicks were raised most years. He noted that the young sometimes try to return to Genesee, but the parents, territorial birds that they are, drive their grown-up offspring away.

Genesee's peregrines starred in "The Return of the Peregrine," a documentary aired on CBC's *The Nature of Things* in December 2001. Aside from this attention, the peregrines have been allowed to hunt and raise their young in solitude.

Sources: Alberta's Threatened Wildlife *and an interview with Bob Joyes. Prepared by David Strand*

$40 per month over their conventional power bill. For every unit of Green Power used, less fossil fuel was used. By the end of 2000, 3,100 customers had signed up.

The first decade of the twenty-first century would herald EPCOR's second

century of operation as a municipal utility. It would also usher in a completely restructured marketplace. With an aggressive expansion plan in place along with a sound environmental policy, EPCOR was well positioned to compete successfully and responsibly in this future market.

AFTERWORD

New Beginnings

. . . . .

2000 – 2002

BY
KEN WARREN

*E*PCOR adapted to Alberta's restructured power market quickly and effectively; just a few years into the new century, the utility had doubled its customer base and vastly expanded its generating capacity. Yet EPCOR continued its environmental leadership and did its utmost to address the concerns of the general public.

BOOSTS TO EPCOR'S GENERATING CAPACITY

EPCOR continued to add to its generating capacity as the new century began. It often cooperated with other energy companies so it could incorporate a variety of different generating technologies into its portfolio. This expansion was part of the utility's strategy to compete in global power markets. Most of EPCOR's new acquisitions were far from the company's traditional Edmonton stronghold, but the company worked to keep its local stations up to date.

A project that the utility began in the 1990s, the cogeneration plant located on the site of NOVA Chemical's petrochemical site at Joffre, Alberta, became operational in the middle of 2000. EPCOR had a 40 percent share in this plant, which had the capacity to produce more than 400 MW of electrical power, as well as steam that is used for the production of ethylene and polyethylene.

On September 15 of the same year, EPCOR and Canadian hydro developers celebrated the opening of the Taylor's Coulee Chute Hydro-electric Plant near Magrath in southern Alberta. The 12.7-MW facility uses water from an existing irrigation canal to generate power. EPCOR also purchased the 7-MW Brown Lake hydro-electric facility near Prince Rupert, British Columbia.

MILESTONES

2000

In January, EPCOR enters into a partnership with the University of Alberta worth $1.125 million dollars.

In February, EPCOR purchases a 7-MW hydro-electric plant located near Prince Rupert, British Columbia.

In March, Canada's Climate Change Voluntary Challenge and Registry honours EPCOR for its leadership in the reduction of greenhouse gases.

In August, EPCOR enters into a partnership with Westcoast Energy to complete a generating station located in Washington. This is EPCOR's first foray outside of Canada.

On September 12, EPCOR acquires Engage Energy's interest in Encore, which is now wholly owned by EPCOR.

On September 13, EPCOR announces an agreement to purchase power from the Weather Dancer wind turbine under construction near Brocket, Alberta.

Taylor's Coulee Chute Hydro-electric Plant opens on September 15.

TOP LEFT: *Taylor's Coulee Chute Hydro-electric Plant near Magrath, Alberta.*

BOTTOM LEFT: *The 7-MW Brown Lake Hydro-electric Facility near Prince Rupert, British Columbia.*

operates at a much higher pressure and temperature than conventional ones. The new design also included advanced flue gas clean-up techniques. This would result in increased thermal efficiency and reduced air emissions. This new unit – designated as unit 3 – will be the first of its kind in Canada. The expansion project was approved on December 21, 2001, and construction started on January 7, 2002.

A GREAT PLACE TO WORK!

Early in the new millennium, EPCOR was recognized as being a great place to work.

Richard Yerema spent two years researching more than 30,000 Canadian companies. The result of his work was *Canada's Top 100 Employers,* a book published in the spring of 2000. In it, Yerema applauds policies and programs that made working at EPCOR more fun and enriching. Noted were a flexible benefits plan and an after-hours career development program. The benefits plan is notable because it allows employees to tailor benefits to fit their individual needs. Under the development program, employees could take courses after working hours, free of charge.

Yerema also praised EPCOR's excellent communications practice. As Don Lowry, president and CEO of EPCOR noted, "We work to keep everyone throughout the organization informed through accurate and timely

All the power generated at this plant was sold directly to BC Hydro.

EPCOR's acquisitions were not limited to Canada. In a partnership with another energy company, EPCOR purchased a partially built 249-MW gas-fired generating plant in Frederickson near Tacoma, Washington. It is scheduled to come on stream in 2002.

As it expanded its interests elsewhere, EPCOR continued to enhance its existing assets. Early in the new century, plans were made to further expand the Genesee plant. This expansion would add about 450 MW to EPCOR's generating capacity. The plans entailed the use of the best technology commercially available: a supercritical boiler, which communications – whether we have good news or bad." Yerema also noted, interestingly, that the restructured market, and the subsequent transformation of EPCOR from a municipal department to a corporation, resulted in a workplace that was more challenging and enjoyable.

ONE OF CANADA'S LARGEST!

In 2000, EPCOR's electricity retail customer base grew by 350,000 from a previous base of 270,000. This was a result of the addition of customers once supplied by TransAlta Utilities. Utili-Corp Networks Canada had acquired the distribution network and retail customers from TransAlta, and an agreement with EPCOR was negotiated. UtiliCorp would continue to own and operate the distribution system, and EPCOR would supply these new customers, unless some chose to exercise their option of purchasing energy from another provider. EPCOR's customer base now covers more than half of the province of Alberta, a far cry from the small town utility of 100 years ago!

As a result of its participation in markets across the province, EPCOR now has a presence in Calgary. The EPCOR Centre for Performing Arts is located in Calgary, along with the Calgary Call Centre and EPCOR Place, an office tower in downtown Calgary.

In October of 2001, EPCOR made another acquisition, one that added nearly 900,000 customers to its base and established the utility in Ontario. EPCOR purchased Union Energy and Westcoast Capital, which were both previously owned by Westcoast Energy, Inc. Union Energy's primary business was renting water heaters to customers, though both it and Westcoast Capital also dealt in climate-control products, servicing, and natural gas sales. This purchase catapulted EPCOR to new heights: it became one of the nation's top providers of energy and related services.

RESTRUCTURING

By January 1, 2001, the electrical market had been substantially restructured. Despite this, there remained a number of temporary measures in place that were designed to help both consumers and generators adjust to the new market. Power-purchase agreements guaranteed sales for generating companies, protecting them from the sudden burden of bearing capital investments they had made under the more supportive old system. A regulated-rate option provided customers with a more stable electrical price than the new market could provide, and government rebates to cushion the combined blows of rapid load growth, hesitant generation development, and escalating natural gas prices. All of these insulating measures were needed as the market was restructured and power rates soared. A definitive verdict on the restructuring process has yet to be reached.

EPCOR'S ENVIRONMENTAL LEADERSHIP

In its second century, EPCOR continued to find new ways to balance environmental stewardship with financially viable electricity production; the super-critical boiler planned for Genesee is one manifestation of this effort. EPCOR's efforts to reduce greenhouse gas emissions led to an award by Canada's Climate Change Voluntary Challenge

CAIRINE MacDONALD

Cairine MacDonald was born and raised in Calgary, Alberta. She studied for her undergraduate degree at the University of Alberta and completed her MBA at the University of Western Ontario.

Cairine joined Edmonton Power in 1997, as vice-president of Distribution and Transmission. She was appointed president of EPCOR Energy Services Inc. in 1999. In both capacities, she was responsible for the transition from a regulated utility to a competitive marketplace and oversaw the utility's electricity retail business. She also oversaw the acquisition and integration of both the customer base and the employees that EPCOR gained from UtiliCorp in late 2000. This acquisition doubled the customer base and size of Energy Services.

Prior to joining EPCOR, Cairine spent 15 years in the telecommunications industry, the last three as

president of TELUS Advertising Services (Edmonton) Inc.

Cairine has been chair of the Canadian Electricity Association — Customer Strategic Issues Working Group. She has also served on a number of voluntary committees and boards, including the Grant Mac-Ewan College Foundation Board, the Citadel Theatre Board, and the Hire-

a-Student Society. She is also an active member of the Rotary Club.

Cairine is married to Bernie.

and Registry in March 2000. Minister of the Environment David Andersen and Minister of Natural Resources Ralph Goodale presented this honour to President Don Lowry in recognition of EPCOR's efforts to reduce greenhouse gas emissions.

EPCOR's environmental policies had to account for its reliance on fossil fuels. Though the corporation owns generating stations that produce "green" power, the company had no choice, for a variety of reasons, but to continue to use thermal generating plants for much of its output.

One of the ways EPCOR compensates for its reliance on fossil fuels is through carbon dioxide emission-reduction credits. Companies better situated to take advantage of "green" power generation opportunities earn these credits by reducing emissions. These credits can be sold to companies, such as EPCOR, that do not have an opportunity to earn them. EPCOR Utilities and Fortum Corporation of Finland announced an agreement in November 2000 to trade energy emission credits. This was the world's largest trade of its kind.

EPCOR's Green Power program received a production boost in the fall of 2001, when the Weather Dancer 1 wind turbine, located near Brocket on the land of the Peigan First Nation, came online.

The 72-metre-high turbine, capable of producing sufficient electri-city to power about 450 homes for a year, was a partnership between the Peigan Indian Utility Corporation and EPCOR.

"Weather Dancer 1 ties the traditional elements of our culture with the goal of development of new opportunities for the Peigan people," said Peter Strikes With a Gun, chief of the Peigan First Nation.

Our success with Weather Dancer 1 is allowing us to look ahead to a larger wind-power project, and a future where it may be possible for us to meet the energy needs of our own community. This will also bring new opportunities for the coming generations of the Peigan people.

The wind turbine was named after a ceremony that symbolizes human relationship with nature; this ceremony is performed at the Sundance. The 900-kW unit was manufactured by NEG Micon of Denmark; NEG had installed more than 7,000 similar turbines around the world at the time of the Weather Dancer commission.

INSPECTORS

Inspections have long been part of EPCOR's business. All municipally approved electrical projects had to be inspected before they could proceed. Some types of electrical equipment also had to be inspected.

As EPCOR moved into the restructured market, and away from its past role as a municipal department, it decided to get out of the business of inspections. It found a way to do this without leaving a gaping hole in Edmonton's electrical industry, or laying off employees who had committed many years to the company. A group of former employees – inspectors all – formed their own company, dubbed The Inspectors Group, Inc., and took over EPCOR's inspection operation in the summer of 2001.

Stan Misyk, president of the new company, said:

All of us are really excited about the future. We have a lot of experienced people who have worked together for a long time. Now we have a new opportunity to use that experience and build on it in our own company.

NEW PARTNERSHIPS

At a reception held on the night of January 26, 2000, EPCOR and the University of Alberta unveiled a partnership between the two organizations worth $1.125 million dollars.

The money, which would be given to the university over five years, would benefit the university's faculties of business and engineering.

The Faculty of Business was to use its share, worth half a million dollars, to create EPCOR professorships in energy policy, regulatory economics, and technology commercialization. The Faculty of Engineering was to employ the balance of the funds to conduct research into fossil-fuel combustion. EPCOR hoped that this would result in technology allowing for more efficient and environmentally friendly coal combustion. Don Lowry noted that this was a field of vital importance to Alberta and to the energy industry, which remained dependent on fossil fuels.

A RELIABLE SOURCE

The Canadian Electricity Association gave Clover Bar's four generating units top marks for availability and production reliability in the year 2000.

The Canadian Electricity Association uses these two measures to rank fossil-fuel burning units. "Availability" refers to how often a machine is available to supply needed power; "reliability" is a measure of how often a machine must be shut down for repairs.

Clover Bar's units spent less time off-line for maintenance than any of the other 86 fossil-fuel-burning generating units in Canada. They also performed reliably and within expectations whenever they were in operation.

In fact, six of EPCOR's units – Clover Bar's four and two of Genesee's generators – ranked in the top ten for availability, while five of the utility's units were in the top ten for reliability.

HOW TO SAVE?

Ever wondered how to increase the energy efficiency of your home? Or have you thought about your water consumption? Conservation can be a difficult problem for many. To assist the public, EPCOR introduced an Internet-age solution.

By late summer, 2001, customers could visit EPCOR's website and complete an on-line questionnaire. Their answers resulted in detailed reports, customized to the customer's actual usage levels, that were available immediately. These reports displayed ways to save money as well as estimated savings.

The website also featured an "interactive house" and a library of material designed to help customers conserve resources.

INTO THE FUTURE

As the pressures of restructuring and marketplace competition mounted throughout the 1990s, Edmonton Power became a corporate identity of its own under the City of Edmonton, with a board of directors and responsibilities to shareholders. The ramifications of this process were not fully evident until the beginning of the new millennium. In just a few years, the utility that had served Edmonton for a century expanded its customer base and diversified its energy production portfolio. At the same time, EPCOR tempered its progress with environmental responsibility and a sensitivity towards its workforce and marketplace. One must wonder what Alex Taylor and the nine others who brought a few lights to the citizens of Edmonton in 1891 would think if they could see the city now.

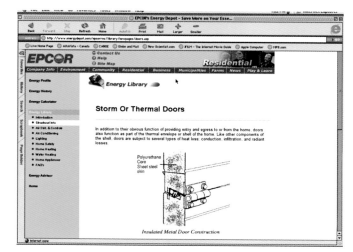

LEFT: *A page from EPCOR's on-line Energy Library.*

Glossary

ALBERTA INTERCONNECTED SYSTEM (AIS)

The interconnected electric system that serves Alberta. The grid includes the generation and transmission systems of EPCOR, TransAlta Utilities, ATCO (Alberta Power), and the City of Medicine Hat, as well as some interconnected electrical loads and municipal systems.

ALTERNATING CURRENT

A current that reverses its direction at regularly recurring intervals of time, and has alternately positive and negative values. In North America, alternating current is produced at a frequency of 60 hertz (cycles per second).

ALTERNATOR

A device that converts (rotating) kinetic energy to alternating current electrical energy.

AMPERE (AMP)

Symbol: A

A measure of the current in an electrical circuit.

BOILER

A device for generating steam that is used in power production (or for other purposes). Tubes containing hot water are suspended in a furnace in which natural gas, coal, or other fuels are burned. In the tubes, hot water is converted into superheated steam.

BUS-BAR

A conductor designed for very large currents, generally in excess of 1,000 amperes, with the capacity to accommodate multiple input and output circuits.

CHLORINATED FLUOROCARBONS (CFCs)

CFCs are sometimes used as refrigerants. They are harmful to elements of the Earth's atmosphere that protect us from damaging solar rays.

CIRCUIT

The conductors that form a path through which an electrical current may travel.

CIRCUIT BREAKER

A circuit-interrupting switch used to control the electrical current in an electrical system, usually located at a substation.

COGENERATION

The use of fuel to produce process heat (steam) in an industrial plant and utilize waste heat to produce electrical energy.

COMBINED CYCLE

The combination of one or more gas and steam turbines in an electric generation plant. Waste heat from the gas turbines is used to generate steam that drives the steam turbines.

DIRECT CURRENT

An electric current that flows in one direction with a magnitude that does not vary or that varies only slightly. Direct current has been used in Edmonton to power street railways, trolley buses, and the light-rail transit system.

DISTRIBUTION

The system of lines, transformers, and switches that connect the transmission network to customers.

DYNAMO
Short for dynamoelectric machine, a device that converts (rotating) kinetic energy to direct current electrical energy.

ELECTRICAL ENERGY MARKETING AGENCY (EEMA)
The Alberta Electric Energy Marketing Agency was established in 1982 to reduce the disparity in electric power generation and transmission costs throughout the province. EEMA was the body that regulated the prices charged to the power distributors.

ELECTRIC POWER
Electrical energy that can be converted to other forms of energy, principally mechanical and heat energy, which is then used to do work or provide light.

ENERGY AND UTILITIES BOARD
A board created in 1995 when the Energy Resources Conservation Board and the Public Utilities Board merged.

ENERGY RESOURCES CONSERVATION BOARD (ERCB)
The Alberta government agency established in 1971 that was responsible for approving transmission lines, generating plants, coal mine development, and changes in service area. (In addition, the ERCB was charged with similar responsibilities for the development of oil and gas resources.)

EXCITER
A source of direct current energy used to create an electro-magnet (rotor) that generates alternating current power in a generator.

GAS TURBINE
Typically, a gas turbine consists of an axial-flow compressor which feeds compressed air into a combustion chamber where liquid or gaseous fuel is burned. The resulting hot gases are expanded through the turbine, causing it to rotate. The rotating turbine shaft drives the compressor as well as the generator to produce electricity.

GENERATING CAPACITY
The maximum amount of electricity a power plant, or generating unit, is able to produce, commonly expressed in megawatts (or in kilowatts for smaller units).

GENERATOR
A machine that converts mechanical energy (movement) into electrical energy.

HERTZ
Symbol: Hz
A unit of wave frequency equal to one cycle (or reversal) per second.

HIGH PRESSURE PLANT
The most recent portion of the Rossdale Power Plant, which contains three boiler-turbine units operating with a steam pressure of 850 pounds per square inch and at a temperature of 900° F. Total steam capacity is 1,980,000 pounds per hour.

HYDRO-ELECTRICITY
Electricity derived from the movement of falling water.

INCANDESCENT LIGHTS
A lamp that produces light by heating a filament to a luminous state.

KILOWATT
Symbol: kW
A unit of electrical energy equivalent to 1,000 watts.

KILOWATT-HOUR
Symbol: kWh
A unit of electrical power equivalent to one kilowatt of energy used for one hour.

LOAD
The amount of electrical power consumed by a particular customer or group of customers, usually expressed in kilowatts (or megawatts for very large customers).

LOW PRESSURE PLANT
The seven boilers and five turbo-generators in the oldest remaining building that housed generating equipment at Rossdale. The Low Pressure Plant operated on the "common header" system and had a total capacity of 1,280,000 pounds per hour at a pressure of 400 pounds per square inch and at a temperature of 750° F.

MEGAVOLT-AMP
Symbol: MVA
A measure of electrical energy equivalent to 1 million volts multiplied by one ampere, commonly used to denote the capacity of large transformers, generators, and transmission lines.

MEGAWATT
Symbol: MW
A unit of electrical energy equivalent to 1 million watts (or 1,000 kilowatts).

METER
A device used to provide an indication of the magnitude of a property of electricity (e.g., current, voltage, or wattage).

OIL-FILLED PIPE-TYPE CABLE (OFPT)
A cable consisting of oil-impregnated paper-insulated copper or aluminum conductors inside a steel pipe filled with pressurized insulating oil.

PEAK DEMAND
The maximum load produced during a specific period of time (15 minutes, one hour, or perhaps 24 hours), usually expressed in megawatts.

POLYCHLORINATED BIPHENYLS (PCBs)
Non-combustible synthetic chemicals, manufactured from 1929 to 1977, used as an insulating material in electrical equipment such as transformers and fluorescent lamp ballasts.

PUBLIC UTILITIES BOARD
The Alberta government agency established in 1915 that was responsible for the setting of electricity rates (as well as other commodity prices, such as milk, natural gas, etc.).

RECTIFIER
A device used to change alternating current into direct current.

RESTRUCTURING
Termination of the government's regulation of aspects of the electrical industry.

RHEOSTAT
A device used to increase or decrease the amount of resistance in a circuit to control or limit the current. Rheostats can be used to dim lights or regulate the speed of ceiling fans (for example), but have largely been replaced by more efficient solid-state devices.

STEAM ENGINE
A reciprocating mechanical device used to change thermal energy into mechanical (or kinetic) energy.

STOKER
A mechanical device that feeds solid fuel into a burner of a boiler.

SUBSTATION
An aggregation of electrical apparatus for the purpose of control, regulation, subdivision, and transformation or conversion of electrical energy. It is the connecting link between two or more sections of a transmission or distribution system.

THERMAL GENERATING STATION
A plant that converts heat energy derived from the combustion of fuel into electricity.

TRANSFORMER
A static electrical device used to electromagnetically transform alternating current energy from one circuit to another. It usually changes the voltage to a higher or lower voltage at the same frequency.

TRANSMISSION
Transmitting relatively large amounts of power from one point (a power plant) to another (the customer or substation) at a voltage of 25 kilovolts or greater.

TURBINE
The prime mover of a generating unit, consisting of a series of curved blades on a central spindle which is spun by the force of water, steam, or hot gas to drive the rotor of an electric generator.

TURBO-GENERATOR
Any generator driven by a turbine.

VOLT
Symbol: V
The unit of measurement of electromotive force.

WATT
Symbol: W
An electrical unit of energy equal to the product of a current of one ampere flowing at an electromotive force of one volt.

Appendix

Year	Capacity (MW)	Name
1920	9.6	ROSSDALE A
1921	4.5	ROSSDALE B
1939	15	ROSSDALE 1
1944	15	ROSSDALE 2
1949	30	ROSSDALE 3
1953	30	ROSSDALE 4
1955	35	ROSSDALE 5
1958	30	ROSSDALE 6
1959	30	ROSSDALE 7
1960	75	ROSSDALE 8
1963	75	ROSSDALE 9
1966	75	ROSSDALE 10
1970	165	CLOVER BAR 1
1973	165	CLOVER BAR 2
1977	165	CLOVER BAR 3
1978	165	CLOVER BAR 4
1989	379	GENESEE 2
1993	379	GENESEE 1

DEVELOPMENT OF THE ROSSDALE SITE

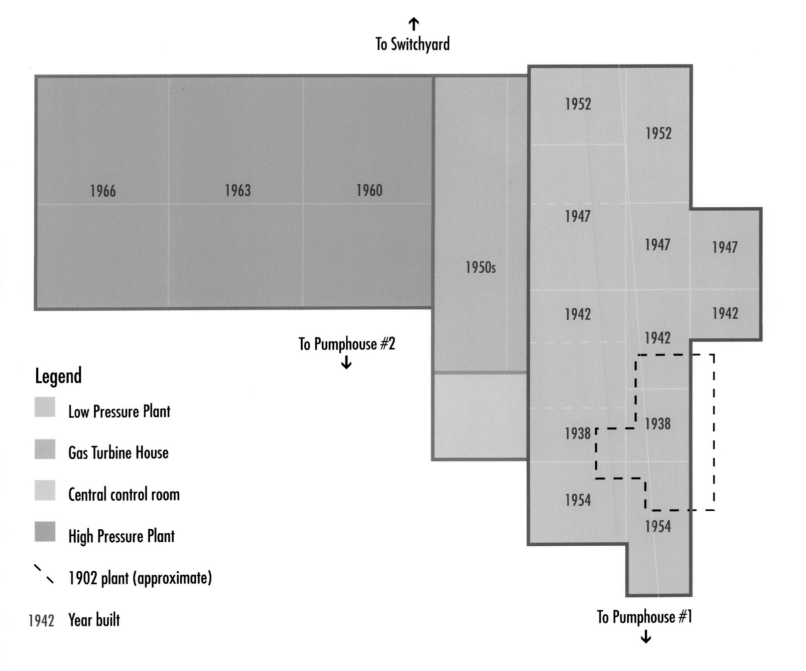

↑
To Switchyard

1952

1952

1966   1963   1960

1947

1947   1947

1950s

1942   1942

To Pumphouse #2
↓

1942

1938   1938

Legend

Low Pressure Plant

Gas Turbine House

Central control room

High Pressure Plant

1902 plant (approximate)

1942   Year built

1954   1954

1954

To Pumphouse #1
↓

Not to scale.

Some demolished sections of the plant are not
represented in this diagram.

POPULATION OF EDMONTON

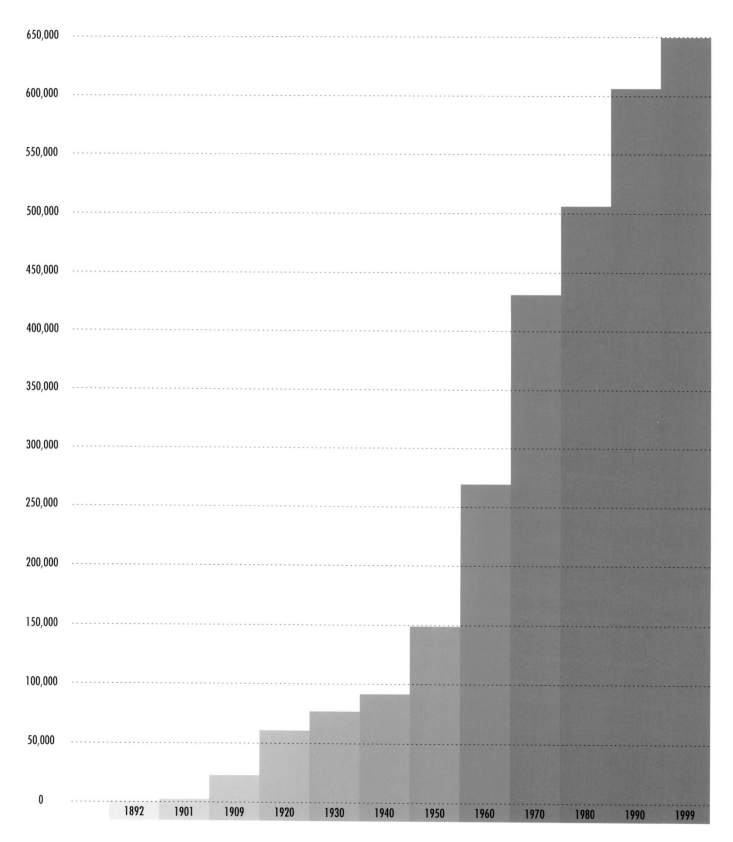

650,000

600,000

550,000

500,000

450,000

400,000

350,000

300,000

250,000

200,000

150,000

100,000

50,000

0

1892   1901   1909   1920   1930   1940   1950   1960   1970   1980   1990   1999

GENERATING CAPACITY OF EDMONTON'S POWER UTILITY

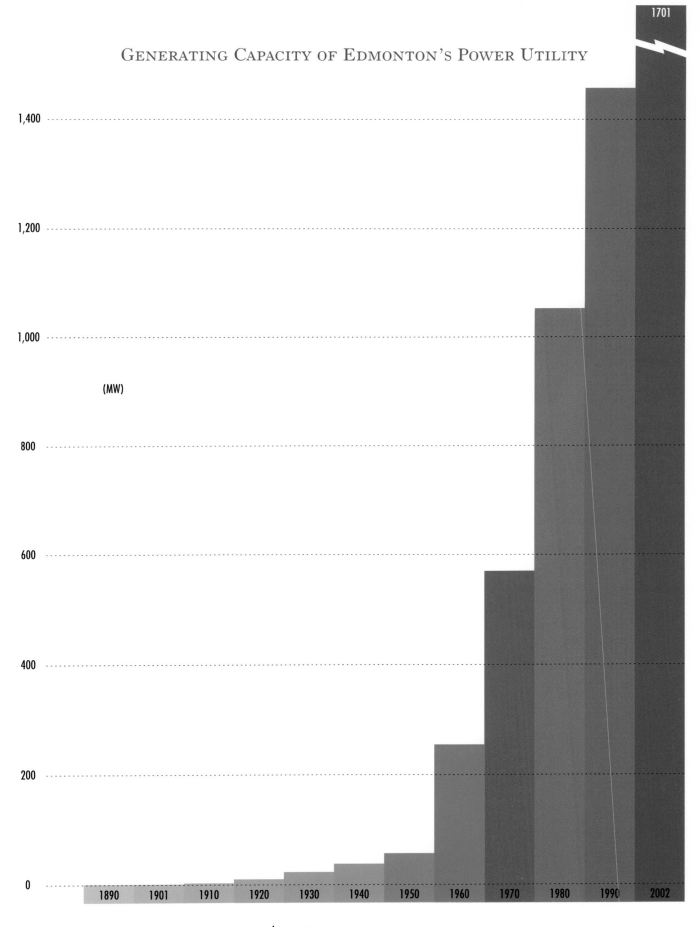

(MW)

1,400
1,200
1,000
800
600
400
200
0

1890 · 1901 · 1910 · 1920 · 1930 · 1940 · 1950 · 1960 · 1970 · 1980 · 1990 · 2002

1701

Bibliography

BIBLIOGRAPHY

General References

Annual reports prepared by the City of Edmonton Electricity Generating and Distribution utility, all years.

Byfield, Ted. *Brownlee and the Triumph of Populism, Alberta in the Twentieth Century.* Calgary: United Western Communications, 1991.

Cashman, Tony. *The Edmonton Story.* Edmonton: Institute of Applied Art, Ltd., 1956.

Dale, Edmund Herbert. "The Role of Successive Town and City Councils in the Evolution of Edmonton, Alberta, 1892 to 1966," Ph.D. diss., University of Alberta: 1969.

Field, Dorothy. "Evaluation of Historical and Architectural Merit of the Rossdale Power Plant," report, 3/1922.

Negru, John. *The Electric Century.* Montreal: The Canadian Electricity Association, 1990.

Person, Dennis and Carin Routledge. *Edmonton: Portrait of a City.* Edmonton: Reidmore Books, 1981.

LaRose, Helen. *The Spirit of Alberta: An Illustrated Heritage.* Edmonton: Alberta Heritage Foundation, 1978.

Chapter 1

p. 2, box: Negru, John. *The Electric Century.* Montreal: The Canadian Electricity Association, 1990.

p. 3, McDougall box: "John A. McDougall's Impact on Edmonton Scene Described," *Edmonton Journal,* 11/1959.
"John A. McDougall Tells Story of the Early History of Edmonton," *Edmonton Bulletin,* 1/2/1918.
"McDougall, Secord Story Impressive," *Edmonton Journal,* 11/6/1963.
"John Alexander McDougall," City of Edmonton Archives document.

p. 4, letters patent quote: 'Old Timer.' "Pioneer Power Firm Served Edmonton Citizens in 90's," *Edmonton Journal,* 16/5/1953.
Alex Taylor box: Person, Dennis and Carin Routledge. *Edmonton: Portrait of a City.* Edmonton: Reidmore Books, 1981.

p. 6, Ormsby quote: "Flood Halted Power Plant for Three Weeks in 1899," *Edmonton Journal,* 8/10/1954.
Walter box: OKM. "John Walter and Mrs. John Walter," Northern Alberta Pioneers and Old Timers Associations document, 1939, 1970.

p. 7, Ormsby box: "Flood Halted Power Plant for Three Weeks in 1899," *Edmonton Journal,* 8/10/1954.
Edmonton Journal article, 3/1961.
'Old Timer.' "The Third Column," *Edmonton Journal,* 5/1961.

General Sources

From *The Edmonton Bulletin:*
"John Walter, Dead," 27/12/1920.
"Alex Taylor is One of Alberta's Pioneer Farmers," 7/6/1913.

∗

From *The Edmonton Journal:*
"John A. McDougall's Impact on Edmonton Scene Described," 11/1959.
"Edmonton's Frank Oliver," 6/7/1960.
"The Third Column," 5/1961.
"Electricity in Edmonton Dates to '91," 12/2/1962.
"Victorian House Now Children's Residence," 1965.
"The Pioneers," 3/10/1982.

∗

Kostek, Mike. "Who Was Alex Taylor?" *Archivist's Corner,* 12/10/1993.

Chapter 2

p. 10, plant box: *The Daily Edmonton,* 16/4/1903.
p. 11, province box: Cashman, Tony. *The Edmonton Story.* Edmonton: Institute of Applied Arts, Ltd., 1956.
p. 12, McNaughton box: "Capt. McNaughton One of Edmonton's Best

Known Citizens," *Edmonton Bulletin,* 8/6/1916.
p. 13, coal box: Agreement between Samuel Moran and Edmonton Electric Lighting and Power, 1901.
p. 14, annual report box: Edmonton Light and Power Annual Report, 1913.
Rossdale box: "World Traveller Found Haven in Old Edmonton," *Edmonton Journal,* 23/4/1955.
"Donald Ross, for Forty-Three Years Resident of City, Dead," *Edmonton Bulletin,* 21/12/1915.
"The Donald Ross," *Alberta Hotelman,* 6/1965.
"Historic Rossdale," City of Edmonton Archives document.
p. 16, signs box: "Electric Signs are Being Discarded," *Edmonton Bulletin,* 23/12/1910.
flood box: "Power Plant and Pumping Station Stood Test: Flats Flooded to First Street," *Edmonton Bulletin,* 27/6/1915.

General Sources

from *The Edmonton Bulletin:*
"Edmonton Gets Offers of Cheaper Electric Power," 8/6/1910. 9/6/1910.
"Will Buy Electric Power at Twenty Dollars per Horsepower," 12/7/1910.
"Looseness at Power Plant, Says Bouillon," 16/7/1910.
"Power House Ready This Fall," 4/10/1910.
"City May Lose Athabasca Power," 13/10/1910.
"Province to Control Power," 26/10/1910.
"Electric Signs Are Being Discarded," 23/12/1910.
"Bouillon Would Not Develop Grand Rapids Power," 26/1/1911.
"Offer Plant for Three Million or Power at Twenty-Seven Dollars," 7/3/1911.
"Matters Municipal," 18/3/1911.
"City May Build Big Power Plant," 21/3/1911.
"Power Company Submits to All Requests of City," 23/10/1915.
"Light and Power Dept. Has Surplus," 17/5/1916.
"Hydro-Electric Work Done by Edmonton Power Co. Is to Be Investigated by Committee," 10/4/1918.

∗

from *The Edmonton Journal:*
"What Hydro-Electric Power Proposal Means to City," 13/11/1915.
"50 Years Ago," 25/2/1960, 4/2/1961, 13/3/1961, 12/11/1962.

∗

"Financial Statements and Auditor's Report for the Year Ending 31/12/1902," report, Town of Edmonton, 1903.

Chapter 3

p. 18, Cunningham box: "Death Takes Street Rlys. Chieftain," *Edmonton Bulletin,* 14/5/1934.
"W.J. Cunningham, Power Tram Chief, Dies Sunday," *Edmonton Journal,* 14/5/1934.
Edmonton Journal, 18/2/1935.
"W.J. Cunningham Sundial Unveiled," *Edmonton Journal,* 30/8/1937.
p. 20, first Cunningham quote: Cunningham, W.J. "Power Production." *Edmonton's Municipal Utilities,* p. 14. City of Edmonton, 1928.
second Cunningham quote: Ibid., p. 12.
p. 23, Murphy quote: Murphy, W.J. Correspondence to Mr. D. Mitchell, 1926.
neon box: LaRose, Helen. *The Spirit of Alberta: An Illustrated Heritage.* Edmonton: Alberta Heritage Foundation, 1978.
p. 24, Mitchell quote: Mitchell, D. "The Story of Edmonton's Municipal Utilities." *Edmonton's Municipal Utilities,* pp. 3-4. City of Edmonton, 1928.
quotes from pamphlet: "Opposition to Public Operation," pamphlet, publisher unknown.

pamphlet box: Untitled pamphlet, publisher unknown.
p. 26, Cunningham quote: Cunningham, W.J., "City of Edmonton Power Department," report.

General Sources

Edmonton Journal, 18/2/1935.

∗

Bell, F. Correspondence to D. Mitchell, 15/5/1934.
City of Calgary. General correspondence relating to power exchange, 1925.
City of Edmonton, general correspondence relating to municipal utilities, 1929.
Cunningham, W.J. General correspondence, 1920-1934.
Edmonton Power Situation, The. Report. 23/8/1929.
Murphy, W.J. General correspondence, 1926.
Pearson, Vernon and John Haddin, "Report on Possibility of Cheaper Power in Alberta," report, 8/1925.

Chapter 4

p. 27, Industrial Association quote: "Festive Streets, Coloured Lights, Christmas Plan," *Edmonton Journal,* 8/11/1930.
p. 29, Cunningham quote: EPCOR document.
p. 30, Cunningham quote: Cunningham, W.J. Correspondence to Commissioner Mitchel, 28/1/1927.
p. 31, wires box: Barnhouse, W. Correspondence to D. Mitchell, 1930.
Shute, A.G. Correspondence to J.M. Douglas, 1930.
Walker, U. Correspondence to A.G. Shute, 1930.
p. 32, Cunningham quote: Cunningham, W.J. General correspondence, 1927.
taxpayers quote: Pamphlet prepared by Edmonton Tax Research Bureau, date unknown.
p. 33, newspaper report: *Edmonton Journal* article, date unknown.
Madame Dey box: "City Power Fails for Second Time," *Edmonton Journal,* 28/5/1936.
p. 34, Rossdale box: Whiting, David. "Historic Resource Impact Assessment: Rossdale Power Plant," report. 25/8/1999.
range box: "Continue Scheme Electric Ranges," *Edmonton Journal,* 24/1/1939.
pp. 33-35, Stone quotes: Stone, Terry. Interview, 1999.
p. 36, meters box: Barnhouse, W. General correspondence, 1935.
swank box: "'600' Designation Said 'Just Swank'," *Edmonton Journal,* 29/10/1938.

General Sources

From *The Edmonton Journal:*
"Record-Breaking Electric Light Surplus Shown," 15/1/1930.
"Edmonton to Be Hooked Up with Hydro Power on July 1; City Lines Are Being Laid," 21/5/1930.
"White Way Lights ... for City Cover Large Area," 23/5/1930.
"Expert Approves $450,000 New Unit for Power Plant," 24/11/1930.
"Council Approves Expenditure of $450,000 at Power Plant," 16/12/1930.
"Submit Tenders Power Equipment; Total $2,500,000," 15/5/1931.
"Cunningham Denies ... Allegations Over City's Power," 9/9/1932.
"Dependence on City's Plant for Power Unsafe, Says Fry," 1935.
"Council OKs Power Plant; Seek Finance," 13/6/1935.
"In Line with Settled Policy," ed., 14/6/1935.
"Figures That Grow Fast," ed., 16/5/1935.
"Mayor Reduces Cost Estimate on Power Unit," 28/6/1935.
"Engineers Answer Clarke Statement," 12/11/1935.
"South Side Power Suffers as Blast Rips Substation," 12/3/1936.
"South Side Draws Full Power Needs," 19/3/1936.
"City to Start on $1,000,000 Power Project," 26/3/1936.
"Sees Danger in Condition of Edmonton Power Plant," 10/4/1936.
"Citizens on Foot When Trams Stop," 27/5/1936.

"Citizens Walk as Power Off for Two Hours," 27/5/1936.
"City Power Fails for Second Time," 28/5/1936.
"3rd Breakdown of Power Plant in Three Days," 29/5/1936.
"Ask Clarification of Power Outlook," 30/5/1936.
"Name 2 Probers Conduct Quiz on City Power," 30/5/1936.
"Power Supply Breaks Cause Labour Protest," 2/6/1936.
"Need of Steady Power Supply," 3/6/1936.
"Mayor Denies State Power Is Serious," 3/6/1936.
"Power Situation Still Unchanged," 10/6/1936.
"Council Attempting to Shift Blame for Power Trouble to Supt. Ritchie, Says Fry," 29/7/1936.
"Four to Report Against Ritchie, Power Official," 30/7/1936.
"Council Must Share in Any Blame," ed., 30/7/1936.
"Ask Dismissal: Find 'Neglect' after Inquiry on Breakdown," 1/8/1936.
"Where Power Responsibility Lies," ed., 3/8/1936.
"Mayor Casts His Vote to Oust Power Chief When Council Divided," 7/8/1936.
"Ritchie Removal Angers Engineers," 7/8/1936.
"British Fair Play Sadly Lacking," ed., 8/8/1936.
"Fair Hearing Was Not Given Ritchie, Power Plant Chief, City Trades Council Charges," 18/8/1936.
"Settlement Near Power Blast," 19/8/1936.
"Power Plant Bids Sent to Committee," 25/8/1936.
"City in Favor $215,600 Sum Power Tender," 10/9/1936.
"English Firm to Tell Terms in Power Bid," 15/9/1936.
"Talking Finances New Power Unit," 26/9/1936.
"Fear Extensions in Power Snagged," 15/10/1936.
"Clarke Blaming Official on Power," 27/10/1936.
"Reach No Decision on Power Scheme," 30/10/1936.
"Reach Accord on Financing $430,000 Job," 20/11/1936.
"Clarke Orders Ritchie to Quit," 24/11/1936.
"Council, 6 to 5, Confirms Removal of Supt. Ritchie Directed by Mayor Clarke," 3/12/1936.
"Council and City Commissioners," ed., 3/12/1936.
"Professional Reputation," ed., 3/12/1936.
"Cite Qualification for Power Official," 8/12/1936.
"To Weigh Requests on Power Position," 12/12/1936.
"Plan to Consider Power Supervisor," 17/12/1936.
"City and Its Power Users," 18/12/1936.
"Sees Two Ways Solve Problem on City Power," 21/12/1936.
"Name RG Watson Power Plant Boss," 22/1/1937.
"$215,000 Turbo-Generator Order Now Recommended," 19/3/1937.
"Purchase Order in England of Turbo-Generator Unit Authorized by City Council," 20/3/1937.
"Power Plant Work To Proceed," ed., 22/3/1937.
"Highest Bid Recommended for Power Plant Purchase," 26/6/1937.
"Power Chief Retains Views on Stoker Unit," 14/7/1937.
"$221,156 Unit Is Purchased for Edmonton Power Plant," 23/7/1937.
"Council Ponders Power Proposal," 23/7/1937.
"Power Decision Brought Nearer by Mayor's Act," 12/8/1937.
"May Widen Duties City Power Head," 19/8/1937.
"$950,000 Power Plant Development Is Under Way to Meet City's Needs," 5/2/1938.
"Unit to Raise Power Capacity to 40,000 kW," 17/1/1939.
"Calgary Power, City to Renew Inter-Connection Plan Talks," 17/5/1939.

*

From *The Edmonton Bulletin*:
"Superintendent Favors Whiteway," 14/7/1930.
"Power Offer Cuts Expense by $120,000," 13/7/1937.
"Mayor Starts Operation $215,000 Turbo Generator," 29/3/1939.

*

Barnhouse, W. General correspondence, 1935, 1939.

City of Edmonton. "City of Edmonton Financial Statements and Reports for Year Ending December 31, 1936."
City of Edmonton Commissioners. "Report No. 1, 1924–1925," "Report No. 5, 1927," "Report No. 6, 1925," "Report No. 10, 1927," "Report No. 12, 1927," "Report No. 16, 1927."
Cunningham, W.J. "Power Plant Extension," report, 1928.
Pearson, Vernon and John Haddin. "Report on Possibility of Cheaper Power in Alberta," 1925.
Ritchie, Alex. General correspondence, 1934.
Watson, R. "Comments on Advantages of Interconnection," report, 1939.

Chapter 5

p. 38, interchange box: *Edmonton Journal*, date unknown.
pp. 38–39, council announcement: "Urge City Speed Power Plans to Facilitate War Efforts," *Edmonton Journal*, 8/10/1940.
p. 39, fun box: "Fun for Boys Costly to City," *Edmonton Journal*, 23/6/1944.
chemical box: *Alberta: Province of Opportunity*. Calgary Power, 1956.
p. 41, "Power House Tour," radio broadcast. CJCA Radio, 3/3/1943.
p. 42, meter reader box: "Two Women Meter Readers Like Their Wartime Work," *Edmonton Journal*, 25/9/1943.
p. 43, Gibb quote: Gibb, R.J. Correspondence to E.C. Manning, 1943.
bomb box: "Bomb Scare Wrecks Meter for City Light Department," *Edmonton Journal*, 7/4/1949.
p. 44, Stone quote: Stone, Terry. Interview, Edmonton: 1999.
p. 46, protest box: "Protest Against the Power Plant," *Edmonton Journal*, 30/12/1948.
sick box: Ainlay, Harry. Correspondence to Mrs. Christopher Spillios, 6/4/1949.
Spillios, Mrs. Christopher. Correspondence to City Council, 2/4/1949.

General Sources

From *The Edmonton Journal*:
"City Council Will Debate Power Plant Fuel Problems," date unknown.
"Edmonton Lights Doused Briefly," date unknown.
"Power Increase Is 19.3 Percent," date unknown.
"Power Firm Head Predicts 'Amicable' Pact with City," 7/8/1940.
"Utilities, Street Cars Stalled by Major Power Breakdown," 12/8/1940.
"Paterson Overrules Watson, Takes Calgary Firm's Offer," 13/8/1940.
"Council Approves Principle New Calgary Contract," 20/8/1940.
"Council Continues Review Proposed Power Agreement," 27/8/1940.
"Council Approves Agreement Hook-Up with Calgary Power," 29/8/1940.
"Calgary Power, Edmonton Units Are Cutting In," 10/9/1940.
"Ottawa Power Official OK's Exchange Plan," 23/9/1940.
"Council Votes 3-Month Delay in $730,000 Power Proposal," 24/9/1940.
"Urge City Speed Power Plans to Facilitate War Efforts," 8/10/1940.
"Council Agrees Place Order $730,000 Power Equipment," 10/10/1940.
"Edmonton Never Pays Cash to Calgary Power in Pact," 11/1940.
"Trams Stalled, Lights Out When Snow Breaks Circuit," 12/1940.
"City Takes Steps to Provide for Power Plant Extension," 19/2/1941.
"First Major Break in 1939, Others Occur Since, Claims," 22/7/1941.
"Power Boilers for 24 Hours," 28/4/1942.
"Edmonton Power Plant Aids War Work in Southern Alberta," 15/9/1942.
"Power Production Increases 27.4%," 4/12/1942.
"Power Output Shows Increase Over Last Year," 22/12/1942.
"New Power Plant Equipment Arrives," 1943.
"City Equipment Is Lost at Sea," 11/1/1943.
"Power Plant Coal Pile Down, Situation 'Extremely Serious'," 18/5/1943.

"Slack Piles at Abandoned Mines to be Brought to City Plant," 4/11/1943.
"City Dimout to Continue," 17/11/1943.
"Power Output Up Despite Dimout," 18/11/1943.
"Power Production Shows Big Gain," 23/11/1943.
"Dimout Shortened by Half an Hour," 25/11/1943.
"Edmonton Dimout Will End Tonight," 25/11/1943.
"Ottawa Approves Civic Improvement," 25/11/1943.
"Reserve at Plant Nearly 3,000 Tons," 1/12/1943.
"City Land Sales, Building Set New Records in 1943," 3/1/1944.
"Steam and Hydro Power Combined," 4/1/1944.
"Large Area Hit by Power Break," 15/1/1944.
"Increase Output at Power Plant," 3/2/1944.
"Output of Power Shows Increase," 22/2/1944.
"Power Production Continues to Climb," 4/3/1944.
"Power Plant Coal Reserve is Large," 17/3/1944.
"New Turbine Installed, Tested at Power Plant," 26/3/1944.
"Watson in East to Check Orders," 26/3/1944.
"Official Pleased with New Turbine," 10/4/1944.
"City Power Plant Revenue Advances," 26/6/1944.
"Output of Power Continues Increase," 30/6/1944.
Articles titled "Power production increases ..." June-November 1944.
"Dimout in City Is to Continue," 22/11/1944.
"60,000,000 KWH Power Owed City," 27/11/1944.
"$169,953 Is Paid by Power Firm," 11/12/1944.
"$1,770,000 Power Project for City Plant Is Asked," 1945.
"Officials Discuss Power Agreement," 14/2/1945.
"Suggests Plan Repayment of Power 'Lent' by City," 9/3/1945.
"Awaiting Details on Calgary Plant," 23/3/1945.
"71,154,200 Hours Is Owed by Firm," 5/4/1945.
"Calgary Power Co. Debt Increasing," 12/4/1945.
"Authorize Study of Power Project," 16/5/1945.
"Work Is Started on Water Project," 19/5/1945.
"Name Committee To Study Power," 19/5/1945.
"Committee Recommends City Sell Power for Rural Users," 6/6/1945.
"Council Approves Selling of Power," 13/6/1945.
"Utilities Profits Show Increase," 21/7/1945.
"Power Developments Urged to Attract New Industries," 30/7/1945.
"$1,770,000 Power Extension Is Authorized by Council," 5/9/1945.
"Another City Power Plant Extension," ed., 6/9/1945.
"Violating a Sound Principle," 13/9/1945.
"Second Bid Seen for City Turbine," 28/9/1945.
"Boiler Is Offered for $579,955 Plus," 7/11/1945.
"Domestic Power Rates Revision," 12/12/1945.
"Ask Council Back Power-Sale Plan," 10/12/1945.
Editorials, 13/12/1945, 9/5/1946, 26/11/1946, 9/5/1949, 20/8/1949, 17/9/1949, 23/12/1949.
"City Lowers Electricity Rate; $286,000 Less in First Year," 3/4/1946.
"Edmonton Said Benefitting by Calgary Power Exchange," 17/5/1946.
"New Power Sale Agreement Is Reported to Council," 25/11/1946.
"Realize $20,000 by Power Deal," 26/11/1946.
"City Utilities' Revenue Gains but Surplus Cut $511,583," 7/1/1948.
"Use of Power Here Sets Record," 6/2/1948.
"Profit $247,028 on Electric Lights," 19/2/1948.
"Power House Extension Brings $1,050,000 Bond Sale," 22/9/1948.
"Power Consumption Shows Increase," 22/9/1948.
"Outlines Growth Light Department," 23/9/1948.
"Mysterious Breaks in Power Baffle," 14/12/1948.
"Protest Smoke of Power Plant," 30/12/1948.
19/12/1949
Report by Commissioners on Power Exchange Asked," 9/1/1949.
"City's Power, Gas Supplies Ample for Current Cold Snap," 24/2/1949.
"Lighting Planned at City Entrances," 1/3/1949.

"Power Consumption Increases in City," 4/3/1949.
"Committee Favors Purchase New City Power Generator," 29/3/1949.
"Bomb Scare Wrecks Meter for City Light Department," 7/4/1949.
"Council Decides to Convert 2 of 5 Boilers to Gas," 7/5/1949.
"Power Generated Up For 6 Months," 11/7/1949.
"Start Conversion at Power Plant," 20/7/1949.
"Main Cables Fail, Power Cut Off," 28/7/1949.
"West End Is Hit by Power Break," 2/8/1949.
"Power Use Up," 8/8/1949.
"City Power Plant 'Largest of Kind'," 11/8/1949.
"Power Plant Smoke Remains Problem," 12/9/1949.
"City Plans $100,000 Purchase of 2 Emergency Generators,"
   16/9/1949.
"Reduction Seen in Ash Nuisance," 8/11/1949.
"Gas-Fired Boiler Cuts Ash Problem," 12/12/1949.
"Street Light Plan Delayed by Shortage of Linemen," 19/12/1949.
"City Plant Aids Hydro," 19/12/1949.
"Recommend Switch of Third Power Plant Boiler to Gas,"
   22/12/1949.

*

"Power Production Reveals Increase," *Edmonton Bulletin,* 7/10/1943.

A.R. Mackay. Correspondence to City Council, 2/7/1943.
"City of Edmonton Electric Light and Power Distribution System, Over-
   head Expenses, Monthly," report, 24/9/1943.
Dick, W.J. "Edmonton Coal Operators Brief Respecting Continued Use
   of Coal as Fuel at City of Edmonton Power Plant," report, 1949.
Ferrier, Thos. Correspondence to City Commissioners, 18/2/1949.
Fry, J.W. Correspondence to James A. MacKinnon, 9/7/1943.
Gibb, R.J. General correspondence, 1943.
King, W.D. Correspondence to R. Gibb, 19/12/1944.
McFarland, W.I. General correspondence, 1947-1949.
McFarland, W.I. Report. 22/4/1949.
Manning, Ernest. Correspondence to J.W. Fry, 19/8/1943.
Menzies, D. Correspondence to Mrs. A. Piersdorff, 11/3/1949.
Parsons, Sidney, J. Hodgson, and D.B. Menzies. Report. 21/12/1949.
Piersdorff, Mrs. K. Correspondence to City Council, 5/3/1949.
"Power House Tour," radio broadcast, CJCA Radio, 3/3/1943.
"Power Outage," radio broadcast, CFRN Radio, 8/1942.
Riverdale Community League. Correspondence to City Council,
   9/1/1949.
Stairs, D., for H.J. Symington. Correspondence to Mayor of Edmonton,
   8/10/1943.
Taylor, W.J. Correspondence to R. Watson, 21/10/1943.
Watson, R.J. General correspondence, 1943, 1945.

Chapter 6
p. 49, *Journal* quote: "City Power Plant Marks Record Year of Production," *Edmonton Journal,* 27/12/1950.
p. 50, Manning quote: *Edmonton Journal* article, 21/10/1953.
p. 51, Faulder quote: Faulder, George. Interview, 1999.
prongs box: "New Electric Plug-Ins Now Required in Kitchens," *Edmonton Journal,* 16/9/1954.
Battistella quote: Battistella, Frank. Interview, 1999.
p. 52, Faulder quotes: Faulder, George. Interview, 1999.
McFarland box: "Power Superintendent W. McFarland Resigns," *Edmonton Journal,* 23/10/1952.
p. 53, oil box: *Edmonton Journal* article, 8/2/1955.
trouble box: Carson, Ed. Interview, 1999.
   Monaghan, C. General correspondence, 1951.
p. 56, OFPT quote: *Edmonton Journal,* 2/11/1957.
p. 57, OFPT box: "'Oil Pipelines' in City to Carry Power Cables,"
   Edmonton Journal, 9/5/1956.
   "Skilled Splicers Work Beneath Tent on City's High Voltage Oil
   Pipeline," *Edmonton Journal,* 31/7/1957.

"Experts to Direct Laying of Four-Mile Oil Cable," *Edmonton Journal,*
   22/4/1957.
p. 59, mayor box: Hawrelak, W. "Meet the Mayor," radio broadcast.
   Edmonton: CFRN Radio, 1955.
p. 60, dangerous box: Lehmann, Waldemar. Interview, 1999.
   Edmonton Journal, 1956, 1958.

General Sources
From *The Edmonton Journal:*
"City Council Urged to Enlarge Power Plant," 1950.
"Power Use Here Climbs 9 Percent," 10/1/1950.
"Name Monaghan Electricity Chief," 10/1/1950.
"Power Substation to Aid South Side," 11/3/1950.
"Extension Planned for Power Plant," 2/5/1950.
"Major Power Plant Addition Said Needed to Meet Growth,"
   5/5/1950.
"Calgary Power Big User of Edmonton Electricity," 5/5/1950.
"Low Tender Said Not Best Offer," 14/8/1950.
"Mine Owners Fear Loss of Power Plant Business," 9/1950.
"Council Fixes Two Prices on Power Plant Coal Supply," 12/9/1950.
"Power Plant Expansion," 18/12/1950.
"Power Plant Unit Sale Is Approved," 23/1/1951.
"City Power Plant To Rescue in Alberta Power Shortage," 3/2/1951.
"Expect City's Power Needs to Outgrow Plant in 3 Years," 3/5/1952.
"30,000 kW Addition Proposed for City Power Plant," 10/11/1952.
"Edmonton Expects to Sell 12% More Power This Year," 23/3/1953.
"60,000-Kilowatt Power Plant Said Considered at Wabamun,"
   23/4/1953.
"Plan Automatic Controls for Power Plant Pumps," 28/5/1953.
23/9/1953.
"City Advised to Expand Plans for Sewage Disposal," 25/5/1954.
"$316,000 Lighting Program Said 90 Percent Complete,"
   17/12/1954.
"Power, Water Plants Grow to Match City Development," 27/1/1955.
"Gas Conversion Plan Approved," 15/2/1955.
"Present Site Recommended for City Power Expansion," 22/4/1955.
"Plant Speeds Expansion to Meet Power Demand," 10/3/1956.
"Power Plant Addition to be Started in Fall," 3/5/1956.
"Power Sales by City Soar," 15/5/1956.
"Fire at Plant Cuts Power," 18/9/1956.
"City Ordering New Generator," 23/4/1957.
"City To Face Building Second Power Plant," 22/6/1957.
"850-foot Power Line Runs Beneath River," 12/11/1957.
"New Gas Turbine Turned On at Power Plant by Mayor," 11/11/1958.
8/5/1959.

*

"Electric Light Department Workshop & Storage Facilities," report.
Kirkland, W. General correspondence and reports to council, 1953-
   1956.
Monaghan, C. "Electric Light Department Workshop and Storage Facili-
   ties: Report to Commissioner Hodgson and Commissioner Menzies,"
   1951.
Monagan, C. "Report and Proposal Concerning the Electric Light and
   Power Distribution System," 29/10/1956.
Monaghan, C. General correspondence, 1951, 1955.
Rossdale Community League. Correspondence to City Council,
   15/1/1955.
Suski, J. "Report on the Organizational Survey of the Power Plant
   Department," report, August 1955.

Chapter 7
p. 62, ad box: Nattall & Maloney Ltd., copy prepared for City of
   Edmonton Electrical Distribution System, date unknown.
p. 63, Faulder quotes: Faulder, George. Interview with author, 1999.
p. 64, sewers box: Interview by Lyn McCullough, 1999.
inspectors box: Interview by Lyn McCullough, 1999.
p. 65, lineman box: Paul, Gary. Interview with Lyn McCullough, 1999.
Journal quote: "Taxpayers' Money At Stake," *Edmonton Journal,*
   1/6/1960.
p. 66, octopus box: "Is there an octopus in your home?" Copy prepared for *Alberta Community Life Magazine,* date unknown.
p. 67, home economics box: From scrapbook collections prepared by
   Edmonton Power Home Economics Department.
p. 68, competition box: Badowsky, Walt. Interview with Debbie Culbertson, 1999.
p. 69, box: Badowsky, Walt. Interview with Debbie Culbertson, 1999.
MacGregor quote: *Edmonton Journal* article, date unknown.
p. 70, curling box: "Oldest Curling Club," *Watt's New,* 10/1970.
p. 71, Kirkland box: Kasten, Henry and George Faulder. Interview with
   authors, 1999.
   "Former City Power GM dies," *Edmonton Journal,* 12/2/1985.
pp. 71-72, Battistella quote: Battistella, Frank. Interview, 1999.
p. 72, bucket trucks box: Interview by Lyn McCullough, 1999.

Works Consulted
From *The Edmonton Journal:*
"City May Turn to Coal if New Plant Built," 5/1/1960.
"Accept $458,580 Bid for Underground Cable," 5/1/1960.
"Nitrogen Dioxide in Plant Exhaust," 24/2/1960.
"Rather Leisurely Studying?" ed., 25/5/1960.
"To Curtail Fumes at Power Plant," 5/1960.
"Taxpayer's Money at Stake," ed., 1/6/1960.
"City Warned on Turbine Low Bid," 23/9/1960.
"City Facing Decision on Building New $12,000,000 Steam Power
   Plant," 24/11/1960.
"Power Plant Building New Intake," 20/1/1961.
"New Turbine Commissioned at Power Plant," 4/2/1961.
"Plan Swap Power Rights," 11/2/1961.
"Report Presented on Power Failure," 2/5/1961.
"Calgary Power Owed City 35,219,800 kWh," 19/5/1961.
"Construction to Start on Power Plant," 8/9/1961.
"Power Plant Coal Proposals to be Heard," 19/9/1961.
"May Begin City Plant by 1966," 20/9/1961.
"Mayor Signs Lease for Coal Rights," 18/10/1961.
"Power Study May Cost $50,000," 19/11/1961.
"Coal Report Expected in January," 25/11/1961.
"Power Plant to Earn City $19,101,000 in Ten Years," 20/1/1962.
"Power exchange deal possible," 31/7/1962.
"Mayor opposing delay in project," 1/10/1962.
"Fumes from Power Plant to Continue," 12/10/1962.
"$112,500 Earmarked for Power," 18/1/1963.
"$50 Million Power Plant Proposed by City for 1980," 8/8/1963.
"Generator Repair Job Under Way," 3/1/1964.
"Workmen's Error Very Expensive," 11/1/1964.
"Power Plant Gas Is Toxic; Danger Denied," 20/11/1964.
"No Room for Complacency," ed., 21/11/1964.
"Power Scheme Rapped," 9/9/1964.
"$227,500 Lost If New Power Plant Approved," 8/12/1964.
"Hazards from Fumes Will Be Investigated," 12/12/1964.
"Tri-City Power Deal May Save $6,840,000," 12/12/1964.
"Ardley Study Bid Renewed," 19/12/1964.
"Hawrelak Will Meet on Power," 2/2/1965.
"Government Crews Begin Ardley Coal Bed Testing," 25/2/1965.
"City Power Officials Test Coal Potential at Ardley," 20/3/1965.
"Ardley Potential Promising," 5/5/1965.

"2 Power Sources Studied," 12/5/1965.

"Pollution Not Due To Brazeau Dam," 12/5/1965.

"Calgary Proposal Will Ruin Ardley, Says Ald. Bodie," 18/5/1965.

""Bodie Favors Power Checks," 3/6/1965.

"Why we ought to keep our power plant AND its reserves," 24/6/1965.

"Natural Gas Use Cheaper than Coal," 8/7/1965.

"City Power Fund Almost Depleted," 8/7/1965.

"Ardley Coal Field Report Termed Negative, Misleading," 14/7/1965.

"Gas Power Plant Urged," 24/7/1965.

"Decision On Power Development Stalled 3 Months by City Council," 27/7/1965.

"City Power Plant Ordered to Clean Up Air Pollution," 7/8/1965.

"Chimney 500 Feet High Needed to Curb Power Plant Pollution," 10/8/1965.

"Air Pollution Menace Here," ed., 11/8/1965.

City Power Plan May Be Changed," 5/10/1965.

"Still Another Shift in Policy," ed., 6/10/1965.

"Power Proposal Given Unofficial Alberta Blessing," 20/11/1965.

"Power Stall Charged as Costly," 23/11/1965.

"Decide, Decide, Decide," ed., 24/11/1965.

"Ross Fears Pollution by Gas Power Plant," 30/11/1965.

"Addition to Wabamun Will Cost $35 Million," 30/11/1965.

"Pollution Study Slated," 3/12/1965.

"Further Pollution Tests Recommended," 15/1/1966.

"They Are Trying to Save Edmonton," 24/1/1966.

"Mayor Optimistic on Gas Tax Removal," 26/1/1966.

"New Coal-Fired Power Plan Before City Council Monday," 12/3/1966.

"Pollution Report Due in April," 19/3/1966.

"It's Cheaper for Province to Buy City Electricity," 19/3/1966.

"Coal-Fired Power Plant Idea Ousted," 22/3/1966.

"East End Will House New Plant," 6/4/1966.

"City Wants Deadline Extended on Pollution Control Proposals," 30/4/1966.

"Pollution Study Extension Likely," 3/5/1966.

"City Power Plant No Pollution Villain," 5/5/1966.

"Further Air Pollution Study to Be Ordered," 25/6/1966.

"Pollution Study Near Completion," 4/7/1966.

"May Begin City Plant by 1966," 20/9/1966.

"Power Plant's Stacks May Rise," 25/1/1967.

"Pollution Rules Not a Problem," 26/1/1967.

"What Air Pollution Problem?" 23/2/1967.

"Pollution Report Expected in May," 28/4/1967.

"How To Prevent Power Halts Sought," 19/7/1967.

"Power Cuts Problem Eliminated," 6/9/1967.

"Gas-Coal Debate Resuming?" 7/2/1968.

"City Taking No Chances on Pollution," 22/2/1968.

"City Jolted by High Costs of Pollution Control Bids," 6/4/1968.

"Stacks Pact Okayed," 22/4/1968.

"Master Control Centre Built for Edmonton's Power System," 31/5/1968.

"Power Plant First of Kind in North America," 13/9/1968.

"Power Returns to City Homes after 14 Hours," 28/2/1969.

"Turbine Repairs Near Completion," 21/10/1969.

"Action in Advance," 5/12/1969.

"Power Plant Turbine in Service," 11/12/1969.

"Power Plant Project Still on Schedule," 30/12/1969.

*

"Edmonton Power Generation and Water Treatment Department," report, 1969.

Gerber, Abraham. "Power Pools and Joint Plant Ownership," *Public Utilities Fortnightly.* 12/9/1968.

"Interruptions to AC and DC Power Supplies between May 18 1961 and June 26 1961," report, 1961.

Kirkland, W. "Future Power Development for The City of Edmonton," report, 18/6/1965.

Kirkland, W. "Report on Exhaust Gases," report, 23/2/1960.

Chapter 8
Direct Quotes

p. 76, explosive box: Viehmann, Willi. Interview with Lyn McCullough, 1999.

p. 78, government announcement: "City Power Rates to Go Up," *Edmonton Journal,* 10/5/1974.

power failure box: "Tension runs high as crews battle power failure," *Edmonton Journal,* 7/8/1973.

p. 79, strike box: Budge, Kelly. Interview, 1999.

p. 80, environmentalist quote: "Coal-burning power plants may be harmful," *Edmonton Journal,* 28/7/1978.

p. 82, substation box: Baird, Art. Interview, 1999.

p. 83, personality box: "Watt's New Personality," *Watt's New,* 10/1970

pp. 84-85, Genesee feature: Pettican, Al and Ken Warren. Interview with Lyn McCullough, 2002.

General Sources

From *The Edmonton Journal:*

"Power Profit a Record," 4/1/1970.

"314 Kites Rescued from Power Lines," 13/4/1970.

"Delay Sought in Final Switch to Mercury Lights," 25/8/1971.

"City to Get Mercury Lights," 1/9/1971.

"Fire Hits Giant City Generator," 6/10/1971.

"Plant Fire Blamed on Faulty Equipment," 12/10/1971.

"$200,000 Blast Cuts Power in City West End," 9/6/1972.

"River Peaks, Flood Threat Over," 28/6/1972.

"City May Apply for Power Rate Increase," 21/10/1972.

"Power Line Route Alternatives Studied," 11/11/1972.

"City Power Revenue Nearly $1 Million Below Estimate," 24/11/1972.

"City Awaits Report on Massive Power Failure," 19/3/1973.

"Blackout Lessons," 20/3/1973.

"Human Error Blamed for Outage," 20/3/1973.

"Blackout Blamed on Human Error," 3/4/1973.

"Cables Blamed in Blackout," 11/8/1973.

"Power Route Change Sought," 8/9/1973.

"Coal for Power Plant," 20/11/1973.

"Power Walkout Averted," 22/11/1973.

"Warning Issued on Coal Use," 22/11/1973.

"City Making New Bid on Power Line Route," 6/2/1974.

"City Electricity Rates to Go Up," 10/5/1974.

"Coffee Breaks, Campfire Songs in Blackout Gloom," 9/8/1974.

"Power Rate Increase Goes to Council," 10/2/1975.

"Power System Pays Citizens," 4/11/1975.

"Genesee May Be the Next Major Source of Power," 28/9/1976.

"Ranchers Simmer Over Power Plan," 28/9/1976.

"Power Plant Start Ordered," 10/3/1977.

"Genesee Project Will Dwarf Rossdale Plant," 4/4/1977.

"Civic Conservation Measures Advocated," 29/6/1977.

"Genesee Farmers Want Good Dollar for Power Plant Land," 16/8/1977.

"Power Line Goes Ahead," 23/9/1977.

"Genesee Residents Will Resist Electric Project," 27/10/1977.

"Genesee Group Ready for Battle," 5/11/1977.

"City Applies for Plant Approval," 13/1/1978.

"Genesee Group Suggests Leasing Land for Thermal Plant," 13/1/1978.

"Plant 'Threat' to Genesee Lifestyle," 27/1/1978.

"More Land Bought for Power Plant," 1/3/1978.

"Power Talk Fuels Anger of Genesee," 10/3/1978.

"Huge Power Plant 'Will Destroy Hamlet,'" 16/6/1978.

"Big Genesee Project Rejected by Leduc," 23/6/1978.

"Coal Plant Bid Will Be Heard," 28/6/1978.

"Genesee Power Plant's 'Low' Cost Touted," 10/7/1978.

"Draglines Compete with Farm Tractors," 10/7/1978.

"Calgary Power Seeks Delay in City Plant," 15/7/1978.

"Group Urges Higher Prices for Land," 26/7/1978.

"Couple Will 'Fight' for Their Farm," 26/7/1978.

"More Conservation Urged," 26/7/1978.

"Coal-burning Power Plants May Be Harmful," 28/7/1978.

"Genesee Plant Hearing Sets Precedent," 7/8/1978.

*

"Conservation Group Backs Genesee plant," *Edmonton Sun,* 6/8/1978.

*

"1973 Year End Report, Safety and Training Section of Edmonton Power."

Battistella, F. "A Summary of the Clover Bar Generating Station," date unknown.

Battistella, F. "An Introduction to the Clover Bar Generating Station," 1970.

Battistella, F. Correspondence to W. Kading, 30/6/1976.

Battistella, F. "Edmonton Power's New Generating Station," date unknown.

"CB34 Project," report.

Dunsmere, A. Correspondence to F. Battistella, 4/2/1976.

"Electric Power Generated and Distributed for the City of Edmonton by Edmonton Power," booklet, date unknown.

"Generation and Distribution," booklet, Edmonton Power, date unknown.

"Genesee," folio, compiled 1976-1978.

Homeniuk, F. "Description of the Extension to Clover Bar Generating Station," report, 1974.

"Interconnected Operation and Power Pooling in North America," report.

Kirkland, W. "Final Summation of Report on Future Power Development," report, date unknown.

"Year End Report - Production Division - 1975, Common to Both Plants," Edmonton Power document.

Chapter 9

p. 88, artifacts box: "Genesee Plant Being Built on Rich Archeological Site," *Edmonton Journal,* 17/11/1982.

p. 89, ERCB quote: *Edmonton Journal,* 12/12/1984.

p. 90, map: Edmonton Power Annual Report, 1984.

p. 93, Genesee box, diagram: "Genesee Generating Station," booklet, date unknown.

p. 94, critters box: "Critters blamed for power hiccups," *Edmonton Journal,* 11/7/1984.

p. 95, Donaldson quotes: Donaldson, Ron. Interview, 1999.

p. 97, blast box: "Electrical blast throws south side manhole cover," *Edmonton Journal,* 23/5/1985.

Walker quotes: Walker, Dave. Interview with the authors, 1999.

General Sources

From *The Carbon Copy:*

"Genesee Project Gets Cabinet Approval," 12/1980.

"Megaproject Begins," 5/1982.

"Genesee Project Full Speed Ahead," 12/1982.

"Genesee Mine Delayed," 3/1984.

"Genesee Update," 3/1985.

"Genesee Power Plant Delay Recommended," 6/1985.

"Reclamation Research Continues at Genesee," 11/1985.

"Moving Ground," 6/1987.

"Genesee Mine Buildings Under Construction," 10/1987.

"Genesee Grid," 12/1987.

"Genesee Operations," 4/1988.

"Genesee," 6/1988.

"Genesee Construction Update," 1988.

"Genesee Dragline Ready for Commissioning," 12/1988.

"Genesee Coal Mine Grand Opening," 2/1989.
"Genesee Awaits Decision," 6/1989.

*

From *The Edmonton Journal:*
"Genesee Plan Approval Vital, Says Utilities Commissioner,"
   31/1/1980.
"Edmonton Power Seeks Line Approval," 9/7/1980.
"Elderly, Poor Top Victims of Utility Costs Increase," 26/9/1980.
"Coal-Fired Power Plant Gets Go-Ahead," 20/11/1980.
"Power Plea for a New Substation," 3/6/1982.
"Edmonton Power Taking the Reins," 11/6/1982.
"Power Rates Get a Boost from Council," 6/7/1982.
"Cost-Conscious Aldermen Pan Truck-Painting Plans," 13/8/1982.
"Power Utility's Logo Will Come in Cheaply," 3/9/1982.
"5 Overcome by Fumes," 19/11/1982.
"Ammonia Fumes Fell 13 Workers," 20/11/1982.
"Debentures for Genesee to Be Issued," 21/11/1982.
"City Goes to Market for Plant," 24/11/1982.
"Power Bills May Surge Due to New Agency," 15/3/1983.
"Genesee Plant Sale Opposed Despite Rates Jolt," 17/3/1983.
"Pooling Is a Power Play," 24/3/1983.
"Genesee Hot Water May Heat Downtown," 15/4/1983.
"PCBs Stored Downtown," 7/7/1983.
"Toxic Chemical Drums a Hazard, Says Ewasiuk," 8/7/1983.
"Ewasiuk Wants PCBS Moved," 28/7/1983.
"Homeowners Win Round with Edmonton Power," 4/8/1983.
"City Will Move Barrels of PCBs from Downtown," 4/8/1983.
"PCB Move to Cost About $12,000," 10/8/1983.
"PCB Open House to Ease Concern," 4/9/1983.
"Plant Delays Would be Costly -- Kyte," 10/9/1983.
"Keep Genesee, Says Demonstrators," 14/9/1983.
"Firms Ask to Burn PCB-Contaminated Oil," 16/9/1983.
"$1.1-billion Power Plant Given Council Go Ahead," 17/9/1983.
"City Is Caught in Bus Squabble," 21/9/1983.
"ERCB Set to Hear Power Delay Case," 27/9/1983.
"Genesee Delay Hikes Price, Costs Jobs — City," 15/12/1983.
"... But Jobs Have Shorted Out," 16/12/1983.
"Reimer Wants Genesee Built," 23/12/1983.
"Mayor Opposes Plant Delay," 11/1/1984.
"Bogle Open to Decore's Case for Genesee Work to Proceed,"
   18/1/1984.
"More Heat than Light in Super-Plant Debate," 11/2/1984.
"Genesee/Sheerness: Both Will Hurt," ed., 11/2/1984.
"Genesee Labor Dispute Resolved," 16/6/1984.
"Work Stoppages May Cost Taxpayers," 21/6/1984.
"Alberta Power Wants Another Genesee Delay," 1/8/1984.
"European Loan Upsets Council," 3/8/1984.
"$249 Million Extra Voted for Genesee," 12/12/1984.
"Christmas in June: Government Gifts," 20/6/1985.
"Cut Rate on Genesee Load to Shave Millions off Cost," 20/6/1985.
"Power Lines Trap Driver in His Cab," 13/7/1985.
"Mellow Yellow Lights Draw Citizen Complaints," 9/2/1986.
"Worker Hurt in Power Outage," 9/5/1986.
"Beware Sizzle of Electricity," 10/5/1986.
"Aldermen Show Interest in Idea of Shipping Garbage to Genesee,"
   2/6/1986.
"Genesee Price Tag Boosted by $102M," 13/8/1986.
"Battle Shaping Up as Genesee Plant Need Questioned," 1/10/1986.
"Genesee Can Be a Benefit," 17/10/1986.
"City Streetlight Conversion Project Expected to Cut Energy Costs by
   $2M," 25/2/1987.
"Calls Flood Province's Phone Lines," 2/8/1987.
"Report Estimates City's Tornado Tab at $9.1 million," 5/9/1987.

*

"Generosity Shines Through Devastation," *Calgary Herald*, 2/8/1987.
"Shattering Force of Wind Described by Workers," *Globe and Mail*,
   3/8/1987.
"Homeless Look for Memories," *Vancouver Province*, 4/8/1987.

*

From *The Edmonton Sun:*
"Power Logo Left on Ice," 3/9/1982.
"Genesee Go Means 7,000 Jobs," 5/9/1986.
"Strike Could Cost City Millions," 4/5/1987.
"Decore Fears Strike," 5/5/1987.
"Genesee Workers Honour Picket Line," 22/7/1987.
"Genesee Protest Renewed," 29/7/1987.
"Work on Genesee Back to Normal," 31/7/1987.
"Plant Could Close," 30/8/1987.
"Genesee Labor Pay Pact Praised," 8/10/1987.
"Genesee Opens at Last," 15/12/1988.
"The History of Genesee," 11/10/1989.
"Genesee Plant Officially Opened," 12/10/1989.

*

"Eltec, A Division of Edmonton Power," brochure, date unknown.
"Eltec Senior Management Meeting #1," minutes, 29/9/1986.
ERCB Hearings, folio, compiled 22/4/1982.
Genesee Approval, folio, 1983. EPCOR Archives.
"Genesee Generating Station," brochure. EPCOR: date unknown.
"River Crossed in Winter," *The Courier*, vol. 7, no. 2, 1983.
Tornado: A Report. Edmonton: Alberta Public Safety Services, 1987.
"Valley Beautiful," brochure. Fording Coal, date unknown.

Chapter 10

p. 101, Vaasjo quote: Vaasjo, Brian. Correspondence to board of directors, 25/6/1999.
p. 102, box: "Seniors, Labour Protest Sale of Utility," *Edmonton Journal*,
   7/1999.
p. 103, council quote: "Council rules out sale of Epcor," *Edmonton Journal*, 16/7/1999.
p. 108, quotes in Phillips box: "New Chairman Appointed," *Hotlines*,
   November/December 1994.
policy box: Edmonton Power 1992 Annual Report.
p. 109, quotes in Lowry box: EPCOR document, date unknown.
gas box: EPCOR news release, 25/11/1999.
pp. 109-110, company announcement: EPCOR document.
p. 110, solar box: Nodelman, Joel, Tannis Tupper, Daniel Shugar. "Performance and Value of Building-Integrated Photovoltaics: A Case
   Study of EPCOR's 13 kW PowerGuard System," report. Edmonton:
   Epcor.
   Nodelman, Joel, Tannis Tupper, Thomas Dinwoodie, Gordon Howell.
   "Epcor's Building-Integrated, Grid-Connected PV System in Edmonton," report. Edmonton: Epcor.
p. 111, environment quote: EPCOR document, date unknown.
peregrine box: *Alberta's Threatened Wildlife*, brochure. Edmonton: Alberta Environmental Protection, 1998.
   Joyes, Bob. Interview with David Strand, 2002.

General Sources

From *The Carbon Copy:*
"Alberta Government Approved Genesee Expansion," 6/1992.
"Dragline Construction Begins," 8/1992.
"Work Progressing on Dragline," 12/1992.
"Genesee Honoured with Ammonite Award," 2/1993.
"Early Memories from Genesee," 6/1993.

*

From *The Edmonton Journal:*
"'Green Power' Lets Epcor Customers Help the Environment," date
   unknown.
"Residents Want Say at Epcor Hearing," date unknown.

"Selling Epcor Bad Business," date unknown.
"City Grapples with Epcor's Future," 21/1/1999.
"Privatizing Power has Dark Side — Report," 27/1/1999.
"Rushing Sale of Epcor a Mistake, Says Report," 18/2/1999.
"Groups Fight Expansion of Rossdale Power Grid," 20/5/1999.
"Archeologists Digging at Rossdale Site Discover Remains of Old Fort's
   Garden Wall," 14/6/1999.
"Down in the Dumps to Find Greenhouse-Gas Solutions," 19/6/1999.
"Council Set to Debate EPCOR's Fate: Sale opposition grows,"
   15/7/1999.
"Council Rules Out Sale of Epcor," 16/7/1999.
"Historical Board Upset at Epcor Plan," 11/9/1999.
"Rossdale Demolition Heading to Court," 16/10/1999.

*

"EPCOR Group of Companies 1997 Yearbook." Presented to Don
   Lowry. 10/3/1998.
GEMCo 1997 Annual Report of the Greenhouse Emissions Management
   Consortium.
"Landfill Gas," report. Edmonton: Epcor.
Nodelman, Joel, Lloyd Bertschi, Cheryl Ciona. "An Integrated Approach
   to Energy Efficiency," report. Presented to Combustion and Climate
   Change conference, Calgary, Alberta. 5/1999.

Afterword

p. 114, Lowry quote: Lowry, Don. Memorandum to EPCOR employees,
   26/6/2000.
p. 116, wind turbine quotes: "Western Canada's Tallest Wind Turbine
   Officially Opens," EPCOR news release, 9/10/2001.
p. 117, Misyk quote: "The Inspections Group Inc. Purchases Business
   Unit from EPCOR," EPCOR news release, 27/6/2001.

General Sources

From *The Edmonton Journal:*
"Epcor Prepared to Meet Competition in Marketplace," ed.,
   12/2/2000.
"Epcor Pushed for Timely Decision on Expansion," 18/4/2000.
"History and High Voltage," 23/4/2000.
"Standoff Over Rossdale Power Plant Makes Mediation Unlikely,"
   1/6/2000.
"EPCOR Sale Raised Again," 18/7/2000.

*

"1994 — A year of change," *Hotlines*, 1994.
"Canada's Top 100." *Maclean's*, 5/11/2001.
"EPCOR Centre for the Performing Arts," EPCOR news release,
   17/12/2001.
"EPCOR's Clover Bar Plant rated #1 in Canada," EPCOR news release,
   17/12/2001.
"EPCOR Launches Canada's First Comprehensive On-Line Conservation
   Tool," EPCOR news release, 1/8/2001.
"EPCOR Utilities Purchases Union Energy from Westcoast Energy,"
   EPCOR news release, 22/10/2001.
"Great Resources Join Forces!" 1/5/1996.
"Million Dollar Strategic Partnership Announced by EPCOR and the Uni-
   versity of Alberta," EPCOR news release, 26/1/2000.
"Organizing for Competition," EPCOR news release, 2000.
Pasnak, William. "Edmonton Power," *Alberta*. Windsor Publications.
"Voluntary Action Plan Progress Report," 1998. Edmonton: EPCOR Util-
   ities.

Many of the works cited in this bibliography can be located at the City
of Edmonton Archives.

Compliments of

The Edmonton Power
Historical Foundation